Dear President Bush

CINDY SHEEHAN

OPEN MEDIA SERIES

CITY LIGHTS

San Francisco

The Open Media Series is edited by Greg Ruggiero and archived by
Tamiment Library, New York University.

Cover photo by David Turnley/Getty Images. See notes at the back of the
book for a detailed discussion of the photograph.

Excerpt of Marge Piercy's poem "The Low Road" printed on pages xx and xxi
was originally published in *The Moon is Always Female*, (New York: Alfred A.
Knopf, Inc. 1980).

Library of Congress Cataloging-in-PublicationData

Sheehan, Cindy.
    Dear President Bush / Cindy Sheehan.
        p. cm.—(An open media book.)
    Includes bibliographical references.
    ISBN-13: 978-0-87286-454-2
    ISBN-10: 0-87286-454-5
    1. United States—Politics and government—2001–2. United States—
Foreign relations—2001–3. Bush, George W. (George Walker), 1946–4. Iraq
War, 2003–5. Iraq War, 2003—Casualties. 6. Civil disobedience–United States.
7. Sheehan, Cindy. 8. Pacifists—United States–Biography. I. Title. II. Series.
    E902.S53 2006
    973.931–dc22

                                                              2006004259

City Lights Books are published at the City Lights Bookstore,
261 Columbus Avenue, San Francisco, CA 94133.

Visit our website:
www.citylights.com

Contents

We still have a choice today: nonviolent coexistence or violent coannihilation. We must move past indecision to action. We must find new ways to speak for peace . . . and justice throughout the developing world, a world that borders on our doors. If we do not act, we shall surely be dragged down the long, dark, and shameful corridors of time reserved for those who possess power without compassion, might without morality, and strength without sight.

Now let us begin. Now let us rededicate ourselves to the long and bitter, but beautiful, struggle for a new world.

—Martin Luther King, Jr., April 4, 1967, Riverside Church, New York City[1]

Editor's Note

Greg Ruggiero

FIFTEEN YEARS AGO IN WESTFIELD, NEW JERSEY, my friend Stuart Sahulka and I decided we needed to do something to try to prevent our country from going to war against Iraq. Operation Desert Shield's deployment of U.S. troops to the region was well under way, but an all-out war still seemed preventable. In 1990 neither the Internet nor cell phones were available to the average person. But with an Apple computer and a photocopier you could really do something. And we did. David Barsamian sent us a transcript of an incredibly powerful, well-argued speech that Noam Chomsky had recently delivered in opposition to our country's build-up to war. We typed the speech into our trusty Mac, designed it so that we—and others—could easily photocopy it, and ran off a few hundred copies in a way that made it easy to fold and staple into a pamphlet.

Editor's Note

With our backpacks full and good friends to help, we went to Astor Place in NYC to hand out the skinny antiwar pamphlets to anyone who walked by, and to drop off bundles of copies with antiwar friends like Allen Ginsberg and Eve Ensler who lived in the neighborhood. A few days later the U.S. began bombing Iraq. We then took the pamphlet to independent bookshops like St. Mark's Bookshop, Revolution Books, and Shakespeare & Co. in NYC, and shipped copies to others like Black Oak Books, Cody's Books, City Lights, Boulder Bookstore, Left Bank, Prairie Lights, Hungry Mind Books, Elliot Bay, Modern Times, Harvard Book Store, and the Wooden Shoe. The independent bookstores acted like a network, each one telling us about another we should call. We called. By April 1991 Noam Chomsky's *On U.S. Gulf Policy* was hitting local and national bestseller lists. The Open Pamphlet Series was born and quickly grew as a Westfield-based movement-oriented operation opposed to war and the social injustices that breed it.

All that happened over fifteen years ago. On September 12, 2005, I had the honor of spending the day with Cindy Sheehan, Iraq veteran Jeff Key, and Alicia Sexton and traveling with them from La Guardia International Airport to Westfield, New Jersey, where they had been invited by Congressman Frank Pallone to speak at an outdoor press conference. On the way there, I interviewed Cindy about her personal journey, Martin Luther King, Jr., social change, and how the senseless killing of her son Casey triggered a prairie fire within her that spread to Crawford, Texas, and from there to the rest of the nation. With the help of Ralph

Nader's nonprofit organization Essential Information, an abbreviated version of the interview was published days later and distributed in the streets of Washington, D.C., during the massive antiwar rally in September. That pamphlet was the seed from which this book has grown.

Peace advocate, movement leader, passionate—Sheehan is all of these things. But after spending last Monday with her I realize that above and beyond all else, Cindy is a Mother. Not just a Mother, but Mom Laureate, Subcomandante Momus, Nobel Peace Mom, Dr. Mom, Jr., Mahatma Momdi, National Mom, World Mom, Milky Way Mom. Which is to say, Casey's Mom. Cindy summons and delivers a message from the unbearable and inextinguishable anguish parents suffers when their children die before their time. Cindy is on a very clear and focused mission; she is not going to stop until she hears the "Roar of Our Nation Waking Up"—the roar of voices, yours and mine, rising together to end war. Until she hears the shouts of joy when the last U.S. solider returns home from occupied soil, she is not going to stop. The book in your hands is her voice. If you listen you can hear the Roar. If you listen, you can hear your name being called out to get involved. This book is dangerous. It's a spark that can start prairie fires. Please use it.

Introduction

Howard Zinn

CINDY SHEEHAN IS RIGHT: WE MUST WITHDRAW our military from Iraq, the sooner the better. The reason is simple: Our presence there is a disaster for the American people and an even bigger disaster for the Iraqi people.

It is a strange logic to declare, as so many in Washington do, that it was wrong for us to invade Iraq but right for us to remain. A recent *New York Times* editorial sums up the situation accurately: "United States military forces remain essentially alone in battling what seems to be a growing insurgency, with no clear prospect of decisive success any time in the foreseeable future." [1]

And then, in an extraordinary non sequitur: "Given the lack of other countries willing to put up their hands as volunteers, the only answer seems to be more American troops, and not just through the spring, as currently planned . . . Forces need to be expanded through stepped-up recruitment." [2]

Here is the flawed logic: We are alone in the world in this invasion. The insurgency is growing. There is no visible prospect of success. Therefore, let's send more troops? The definition of fanaticism is that when you discover that you are going in the wrong direction, you call it a "noble cause" and double your speed. Our president calls it "staying the course."

In all of this there is an unexamined premise: that military victory would constitute "success."

Conceivably, the United States, possessed of enormous weaponry, might finally crush the resistance in Iraq. The cost would be great. Would that be a "success"? Already, tens of thousands, perhaps hundreds of thousands, have lost their lives—and we must not differentiate between "their" casualties and "ours" if we believe that all human beings have an equal right to life.

In 1967, the same arguments that we are hearing now were being made against withdrawal in Vietnam. The United States did not pull out its troops for six more years. During that time, the war killed at least one million more Vietnamese and perhaps 30,000 U.S. military personnel.

We must stay in Iraq, it is said again and again, so that we can bring stability and democracy to that country. Isn't it clear that after years of war and occupation we have brought only chaos and violence and death to that country, not any recognizable democracy?

Can democracy be nurtured by destroying cities, by bombing, by driving people from their homes?

There is no certainty as to what would happen in our absence. But there is absolute certainty about the result of our presence—escalating deaths on both sides.

The loss of life among Iraqi civilians is especially startling. In November 2004, the British medical journal *The Lancet* reported that up to 100,000 civilians had died so far as a result of the war, many of them children.[3] As of early 2006, the casualty toll on the American side included more than 2,200 deaths and thousands of maimed soldiers, some losing limbs, others blinded.[4] Tens of thousands more are facing psychological damage in the aftermath.

Have we learned nothing from the history of imperial occupations, all pretending to help the people being occupied?

The United States, the latest of the great empires, is perhaps the most self-deluded, having forgotten that history of occupations, including our own: our fifty-year occupation of the Philippines, our long occupation of Haiti (1915–1934) and of the Dominican Republic (1916–1924), our military intervention in Southeast Asia, and our repeated interventions in Nicaragua, El Salvador, and Guatemala.

Our military presence in Iraq is making us less safe, not more so. It is inflaming people in the Middle East, and thereby magnifying the danger of terrorism. Far from fighting "there rather than here," as President Bush has claimed, the occupation increases the chance that enraged infiltrators will strike us here at home.

As things gets worse for ordinary Iraqis and for the U.S. occupation forces, President Bush continues to assure us that the war is winnable, and that it is being fought for a "noble cause."

The fact is, however, however, that Iraq is clearly not a liberated country, but an occupied country. We became familiar with that term during the second world war. We talked of German-occupied France, German-occupied Europe. And after the war we spoke of Soviet-occupied Hungary, Czechoslovakia, Eastern Europe. It was the Nazis, the Soviets, who occupied countries. The United States liberated them from occupation.

Now we are the occupiers. True, we liberated Iraq from Saddam Hussein, but not from us. Just as in 1898 we liberated Cuba from Spain, but not from us. Spanish tyranny was overthrown, but the U.S. established a military base in Cuba, as we are doing in Iraq. U.S. corporations moved into Cuba, just as Bechtel and Halliburton and the oil corporations are moving into Iraq. The U.S. framed and imposed, with support from local accomplices, the constitution that would govern Cuba, just as it has drawn up, with help from local political groups, a constitution for Iraq. Not a liberation. An occupation.

And it is an ugly occupation. On August 7, 2003, the *New York Times* reported that General Sanchez in Baghdad was worried about the Iraqi reaction to occupation. Pro-U.S. Iraqi leaders were giving him a message, as he put it: "When you take a father in front of his family and put a bag over his head and put him on the ground, you have had a significant adverse effect on his dignity and respect in the eyes of his family."[5] (That's very perceptive.)

Introduction

We know that fighting during the U.S. offensive in November 2004 destroyed three-quarters of the town of Fallujah (population 360,000), killing hundreds of its inhabitants. The objective of the operation was to cleanse the town of the terrorist bands acting as part of a "Ba'athist conspiracy."

But we should recall that on June 16, 2003, barely six weeks after President Bush had claimed victory in Iraq, two reporters for the Knight Ridder newspaper group wrote this about the Fallujah area: "In dozens of interviews during the past five days, most residents across the area said there was no Ba'athist or Sunni conspiracy against U.S. soldiers, there were only people ready to fight because their relatives had been hurt or killed, or they themselves had been humiliated by home searches and road stops. . . ."[6] One woman quoted in the article described how U.S. soldiers arrested her husband from their home because of empty wooden crates that they had bought for firewood. She exclaimed that it is the U.S. who is guilty of terrorism.

Soldiers who are set down in a country where they are told they will be welcomed as liberators and find that they are surrounded by a hostile population become fearful and trigger-happy. On March 4, 2005, nervous, frightened GIs guarding a roadblock fired on Italian journalist Giuliana Sgrena, who had just been released by kidnappers, and an intelligence service officer, Nicola Calipari, whom they killed.

We have all read reports of U.S. soldiers angry at being forced to stay longer in Iraq. Such sentiments are becoming known to the U.S. public, as are the feelings of many deserters who are refusing to return to Iraq after home leave. In May 2003 a Gallup poll reported that only 13 percent of the U.S. public thought the war was going badly. According to a poll published by the *New York Times* and CBS News on June 17, 2005, 51 percent thought that the United States should not have invaded Iraq or become involved in the war. When Cindy Sheehan was camped outside of George Bush's vacation home in Crawford, Texas, Bush's disapproval rating was up to 57 percent. By October 2005, 64 percent disapproved of Bush's handling of the situation.[7]

But more ominous, perhaps, than the occupation of Iraq is the occupation of the United States. I wake up in the morning, read the newspaper, and feel that we are an occupied country, that some alien group has taken over. I wake up thinking: the U.S. is in the grip of a President surrounded by thugs in suits who care nothing about human life abroad or here, who care nothing about freedom abroad or here, who care nothing about what happens to the earth, the water, or the air, or what kind of world will be inherited by our children and grandchildren.

More Americans are beginning to feel, like the soldiers in Iraq, that something is terribly wrong. More and more every day the lies are being exposed. And then there is the largest lie, that everything the U.S. does is to be pardoned because we are engaged in a "war on terrorism," ignoring the fact that war is itself terrorism, that barging into homes and taking away people and subjecting them to torture is terrorism, that invading and bombing other countries does not give us more security but less.

The Bush administration, unable to capture the perpetrators of the September 11 attacks, invaded Afghanistan, killing thousands of people and driving hundreds of thousands from their homes. Yet it still does not know where the main criminals are. Not knowing what weapons Saddam Hussein was hiding, it invaded and bombed Iraq in March 2003, disregarding the UN, killing thousands of civilians and soldiers, and terrorizing the population; and not knowing who was and was not a terrorist, the U.S. government has imprisoned hundreds of people at Guantánamo Bay under such conditions that eighteen have tried to commit suicide, and hundreds have gone on hunger strike.

The *Amnesty International Report* 2005 notes: "Guantánamo Bay has become the gulag of our times. . . . When the most powerful country in the world thumbs its nose at the rule of law and human rights, it grants a license to others to commit abuse with impunity."

The "war on terrorism" is not only a war on innocent people in other countries; it is a war on the people of the U.S.: on our liberties, on our standard of living. The country's wealth is being stolen from the people and handed over to the superrich. The lives of the young are being stolen.

The Iraq War will undoubtedly claim many more victims, not only abroad but also on U.S. territory. The Bush administration maintains that, unlike the Vietnam War, this conflict is not causing many casualties. True enough, fewer than 2,000 service men and women have lost their lives in the fighting. But when the war finally ends, the number of its indirect victims, through disease or mental disorders, will increase steadily. After the Vietnam War, veterans reported congenital malformations in their children caused by Agent Orange.

Officially there were only a few hundred losses in the Gulf War of 1991, but the U.S. Gulf War Veterans Association has reported 8,000 deaths in the past ten years. Some 200,000 veterans, out of 600,000 who took part, have registered a range of complaints due to the weapons and munitions used in combat. We have yet to see the long-term effects of depleted uranium on those currently stationed in Iraq. About 200,000 of the 600,000 veterans of the Gulf War filed complaints about illnesses incurred from the weapons our government used in the war.[8] In the current war, how many young men and women sent by Bush to liberate Iraq will come home with related illnesses?

What is our job? To point all this out.

Human beings do not naturally support violence and terror. They do so only when they believe their lives or country are at stake. These were not at stake in the Iraq War. President Bush lied to the American people about Saddam Hussein and his weapons. And as people learn the truth—as happened in the course of the Vietnam War—they will turn against the government. We who are for peace have the support of the rest of the world. The United States cannot indefinitely ignore the ten million people who protested around the world on February 15, 2003.

We ten million are still here. From time to time the inspired among us do not wait for the next mass mobilization to engage in acts of open protest and civil disobedience. These are our truly principled citizens who stand up to the government and remind us that there is no act too small, no act too bold. Such was the case with Casey Sheehan's mom, Cindy Sheehan, when she learned that Casey had been killed in action in Iraq on April 4, 2004. It was only his fifth day in Iraq.

The Sheehans' story reminds us of the age-old truth that in the struggle for a better world everything we do matters. After receiving news of Casey's death, Cindy was frozen with anguish, despair, and a sense of meaninglessness. When her daughter Carly wrestled her own grief into words and wrote a poem about the tragedy, the broken pieces of pain within Cindy began crystallizing into the ethical outrage and sense of civic mission that has energized the peace and social justice movement and sent shock waves beneath the White House, the Pentagon, and every military recruitment center in this country. That age-old lesson, that everything matters, is the meaning of the Sheehans' story, and the purpose of this inspiring book.

A box cutter can bring down a tower. A poem can build up a movement. A pamphlet can spark a revolution. This book, made in the U.S.A. from pain and love, was conceived, written, and designed to end the war.

The significance of Cindy Sheehan and Hart Viges and the 9,999,998 other people around the world is that we exist, we openly resist, and our numbers are growing every day. Some of us, like Carly Sheehan, write poems; some of us, like Joan Baez, sing songs; some of us, like Cindy Sheehan, camp outside the president's vacation home for a month; some of us, like Rosa Parks, sit in the front of a segregated bus; some of us, like Henry David Thoreau, refuse to pay taxes; some of us, like Hart Viges, speak out; some paint; some teach; some bang pots and pans like our friends in Barcelona, some just bring it up at the dinner table. Working together, ordinary people can become extraordinarily strong.

As Marge Piercy writes in her beautiful poem, "The Low Road":

> . . . two people fighting
> back to back can cut through
> a mob, a snake-dancing file
> can break a cordon, an army
> can meet an army.
>
> Two people can keep each other
> sane, can give support, conviction,
> love, massage, hope, sex.
> Three people are a delegation,
> a committee, a wedge. With four
> you can play bridge and start
> an organization. With six
> you can rent a whole house,
> eat pie for dinner with no
> seconds, and hold a fund raising party.
> A dozen make a demonstration.

A hundred fill a hall.
A thousand have solidarity and your own newsletter;
ten thousand, power and your own paper;
a hundred thousand, your own media;
ten million, your own country.

It goes on one at a time,
it starts when you care
to act, it starts when you do
it again and they said no,

it starts when you say We
and know you who you mean, and each
day you mean one more.

We need to engage in whatever nonviolent actions appeal to us.
The history of social change is the history of millions of actions,
small and large, coming together at points in history and creating a power that governments cannot suppress.

Foreword

Hart Viges

MY NAME IS HART VIGES. I'D LIKE TO TELL YOU A LITTLE about my experience as a U.S. soldier in Iraq, and why I am now a conscientious objector against the war. September 11 happened. The next day I was in the recruiting office telling them, "Give me Airborne, give me Infantry." I thought that was the way I could do something hard core to make a difference in the world for the better.

So I went to infantry school and jump school and I was deployed to the Middle East with my unit of the 82nd Airborne Division. We arrived in Kuwait in February 2003.

We drove into Iraq because Third Infantry Division was ahead of schedule, and so we did not need to jump into Baghdad by air.

As we drove into the Iraqi town of Al-Samawa to secure their supplies, my mortar platoon dropped numerous rounds on the town. I watched Kiowa attack helicopters fire hellfire missile after hellfire missile. I saw a C130 Spectre gunship—I don't know if you know what that is, but it can level a town.[1] It had belt-fed artillery rounds pounding with these super-Gatling guns. Laser fire just raining down on the town.

I don't know how many innocents I killed with my mortar rounds. I have my imagination to pick at my brain for that one. But I clearly remember the call-out over the radio saying, "Green light on all taxi cabs. The enemy is using them for transportation."

One of our snipers called back on the radio saying "Excuse me, but did I hear that order correctly? Green light on all taxi cabs?"

"Roger that, soldier. You'd better start buckling up."

All of a sudden the city just blew up. It didn't matter if there was an innocent in a taxi cab, we laid a mortar round on it. We didn't care if there was a child in a cab—our snipers opened up.

Next was Fallujah, April 2003. We went into that town without a shot. But Charlie Company decided they were going to take over a school as an area of operations. Protesters would come up to us and say, "Please get out of our school. Our children need this school. We need education."

Charlie Company turned them down. Local people came back to us in groups of about around forty to fifty people. Some of them had the bright idea of squirting AK-47s up into the air. Well, a couple of their rounds came back down into the school. Charlie Company then just laid to waste to that group of people.

After that we had to get out of there real quick.

Then we went to Baghdad. In Baghdad I had days that I don't want to remember. I try to forget.

We'd take foreign contractors out to a water treatment plant outside of Baghdad—sorry to tell you they weren't Iraqi citizens rebuilding their own country.

We'd caught word that it was kind of a scary place that we were heading to, but when we arrived I saw that it was beautiful—grass and palm trees with a river running through it. There were farmers. It was actually the first beautiful place that I saw in Iraq that seemed untouched by the war.

I'm a good soldier. I watch my sector. I know a distraction can kill you as quickly as a bullet.

As we were beginning to leave, men with rocket-propelled grenades (RPGs) suddenly came running out at us. For some strange reason two men with RPGs ran up in front of us from across the road. They ran over to the right.

I was watching my sector but there was all this yelling over there, over to the right. "Drop your weapons!" "Drop your weapons!" we yelled in Arabic, "Drop your weapons!"

The two men then grabbed women and kids, you know, so we couldn't fire at them. I couldn't take it anymore and swung my gun over in their direction. I locked my sight on one man's chest, my finger on the trigger. I'm trained to kill but I thought to myself, this is no bogey man, no monster, no enemy. These are human beings just like me, with the same fears and doubts and worries, in the same messed-up situation.

I didn't pull the trigger.

It threw me off. In training they never tell you about the emotions that come with killing. They didn't tell me about that. They tried to numb me, they tried to strip my humanity. They tried to tell me that he's not a human being, it's a *soft target*.

So there I was in this situation with my imagination running wild: What if he pulled his trigger? How many American soldiers, Iraqi police, or families might get killed because I didn't pull my trigger?

After we got out of this little village the attack helicopters arrived—Apaches—plus two Bradley fighting vehicles. So we went back to the nice little town, this beautiful town. We start asking questions. "Where are they?" Eventually we were led to a hut where a family was living. With Apache helicopters flying above us, our Bradley fighting vehicles covering our flanks, Mark 19 automatic grenade launchers on our Humvees, and machine guns behind us covering our back, another soldier and I jumped out and approached the hut.

I went in and searched the hut for AK-47s, for explosives, for RPGs, for something that could convict someone, maybe, of a crime. Evidence. All I could find was a tiny little pistol, probably to scare off thieves who were trying to steal their crops.

Well, because of that pistol we took their two young men. Their mother was trying to kiss my feet like I deserved my feet to be kissed. She was screaming, pleading.

I knew what she was feeling. I did not need to speak Arabic to know love and concern and fear. I had my attack helicopter behind me, my Bradley fighting vehicle, my armor, my M4 semi-automatic with laser sight. There I was: an 82nd Airborne killer.

But I was powerless. I could not do a thing to ease that woman's pain.

We spent a year in Iraq. Then we went to Fort Bragg for two weeks. After that I had two weeks' leave to go back home.

During my leave I was able to better analyze what I had been experiencing in Iraq. I came to realize that we've got to make better choices.

My mom took me to the Chicken Farm Art Center and I met new people. Up to that point, the only thing that was holding me onto the war was that we got rid of Saddam Hussein. One day when I was at the art center I heard a woman criticize U.S. policy and say that Saddam was our guy—that the U.S. gave him weapons and supported him. Hearing her deeply affected me.

Then I went to Seattle and saw the film *The Passion of the Christ* with some friends. This deeply affected me too. Even when Jesus was attacked, he prayed in his heart for the well-being of his enemies. I realized that to be a Christian I couldn't go back and kill. I couldn't go back to the war.

At first I didn't tell anyone how I felt. I wore a mask. Then I started to have chest pains. When my friends would tell me about some people they killed or beat up in Iraq the pains would be so sharp that I thought I was having a heart attack. It was hard to breathe. My arm got numb. I went to the doctor. I had blood tests, X rays, everything. The doctor told me that the sac around my heart was inflamed. He gave me anti-inflammation pills and told me to get some rest.

When I got back to my unit I told them about my condition. They asked if I was stressed. I told them that I was—I was stressed. I couldn't lie to them. I told them the truth. I broke down. Everything just flooded out of me. I told them that I just couldn't do it anymore. I just couldn't do it anymore. And the sergeant asked, "What can't you do anymore?" And I told them that I can't pull the trigger. I can't do it. And I remember thinking to myself, they are *really* going to fuck me up. But they didn't.

I went to the chaplain and told him my whole story. He asked if I wanted to file as a conscientious objector. At the time I didn't even know what that was. The words sounded correct in my head. I then went online and researched what it means. Then I contacted a Quaker peace house and got an information packet. I bought a laptop and began working on my application.

Meanwhile, the sergeant and the chaplain helped by having me transferred from a mortar platoon to being a chaplain's assistant. This allowed me more time to work on the application than if I had been out in the field. It took about ten months for my application to be processed and approved.

In December 2004 I received my honorable discharge. I had a hard time adjusting. I couldn't express anything, I couldn't express love. All my relationships were falling apart because they couldn't fucking understand me. How could they know the pain that I've gone through or the sights that I've seen, the dead bodies? The innocence gone, stripped, dead?

I couldn't stand the pain. People were leaving me. I was alone. But I couldn't cut my wrists, I couldn't do it myself. So I called the police. They came stomping through my door. I had my knife in my hand. "Shoot me. Shoot me."

All of a sudden I became the man with the RPG with all the guns pointed at him. Misled, miseducated, thinking that "yes, we can solve all the world's problems by killing each other." How insane is that?

Lucky enough I lived through that episode as well. See, you can't wash your hands of blood with more blood. It's impossible; the wounds carry on.

I learned about Veterans for Peace and received e-mails from them. I was new to the peace movement. I remember hearing this mother talk about her son's killing in Iraq. I remember her voice. She was really pissed off. It was Cindy Sheehan. I heard about her going to Crawford to protest the war. I was in Austin at the time, and decided to go to support her protest.

When I got to Crawford I found this spark, this energy. It's the force that could end the war. It was an amazing gathering of people from all over the country coming together to spread peace. People even came up from Mexico.

Every day we have to make choices. Young people who are thinking about joining the military have to realize that war is not a video game, not a movie. Your best friend may die right next to you. You might have to kill people. If you survive, the fact that you killed people is something that will haunt you for the rest of your life. The uncertainty of wondering if you killed a child or a man or a woman who had nothing to do with the war will haunt you for the rest of your life.

Let me say that again: more Vietnam veterans killed themselves when they came home than when they were in Vietnam. This is what war does to your soul, to your humanity, to your family.

Creation is more powerful than destruction. Trying to find understanding is not something that will haunt you for the rest of your life, it is something that will empower you for the rest of your life. If you want to do something hardcore to help your country and make the world a better place, study Gandhi, study Martin Luther King. These are the kinds of men who are hardcore for me now.

Cindy Sheehan is hard core for peace. Just like Rosa Parks, Cindy Sheehan is a spark for this movement. She is the one who keeps saying to the country, we have to stop this war now, what are we doing sitting around? She is an amazing person—not only is she bringing her pain out to bear, letting everyone know that there are thousands of other mothers going through what she is going through, but she is also showing the country how war destroys the family. She is showing this country that families are losing their children for a lie. That is one of the hardest things to comes to terms with, but it's what Cindy is good at, and that is why everyone in this country should read this book.

Dear President Bush

Conversation with Cindy Sheehan and Greg Ruggiero
conducted en route from New York City to Westfield, New Jersey

Your recent article on Common Dreams' website refers to a speech that Dr. Martin Luther King, Jr. gave on April 4, 1967, at Riverside Church in New York City. In the speech, Dr. King spoke passionately against the military-industrial complex and the machinery of war. Do you think that the U.S. war machine has changed much since Dr. King gave his prophetic speech?

The only thing that has changed is that it has gotten much worse. What our children are dying for is to make the government's war machine rich. The U.S. government wastes billions of dollars each year paying for past, current, and future wars, while U.S. corporations lead the world in selling weapons of death to other countries.[1] We've seen the stated enemies of our country shift from the Cold War to the War on Terror, from the communists to the terrorists, but the results are the same. War profiteers are getting rich off of killing our children—feeding on our young. The war profiteers are our true enemies. The war machine always kills our children, and we, as moms and parents, should refuse to give our children up to them.

At Riverside Church Dr. King also spoke about the young people who have become angry, desperate, rejected—who are so fed up with the system and want change so deeply that they consider moving beyond civil disobedience. They asked King, "If our country can use violence to make its demands with Vietnam, why can't we?" King goes on to say, "Their questions hit home, and I knew that I could never again raise my voice against the violence of the oppressed in the ghettos without having first spoken clearly to the greatest purveyor of violence in the world today: my own government. For the sake of those boys, for the sake of this government, for the sake of the hundreds of thousands trembling under our violence, I cannot be silent." But he goes on to restate his conviction that meaningful social change can only come from nonviolent resistance. What is your thought on the tactics and goals in doing movement work to change brutal government policies?

I am with Dr. King. We must rise above using violence as a means of change. If we want our country to be peaceful we must be peaceful ourselves. If we use violence, then we promote violence. If we use violence, we lower ourselves to the level of our current government. Using violent methods, any movement we organize toward peace will only be temporary. Look at Vietnam; we ended that war but the government started new ones, and now it's started another one in Iraq. I don't know much about strategies, but I do know this: we need to embody the goals that we're struggling for. The only way to build peace is through peaceful means, and we need to do everything we can to oppose this war through nonviolent resistance.

Dr. King repeatedly asserts his commitment to resistance through non-violent means, but he also makes a call for a "positive revolution of values." What do you think that means for us today?

Values. . . . George Bush is always saying that he is a Christian man. I believe a Christian person does not murder people. Jesus was a *prince of peace.* But when you look at the damage that the religious right has done to this country. . . . Those of us who are Christian need to go back to our core gospel values and teach George Bush: *Thou Shalt Not Kill.*

We need to change the whole value system we're operating under. People have been drawn to George Bush because they thought he was making them more secure, but the fact is that George Bush is making our world *less* secure. You don't promote peace by killing people; you don't make people free by killing them. We need to start putting problem-solving and diplomacy before everything else. War is barbaric, and it takes patience, love, wisdom, and brains to avert war, but it can almost always be done.

We need to replace neglect and apathy toward our people—and militarism toward the world—with love, with community, with respect, with equality, with education, with cooperation, with diplomacy. We need to explore new paradigms of peace and democracy that are based on justice, truth, cooperation, and community.

At Riverside Church Dr. King also declared his belief that the Vietnam lar was a symptom of deeper underlying "social maladies." Do you feel that's true today regarding the wars the U.S. is waging in Iraq and around the world?

That's a hard question to answer. I admire Martin Luther King, Jr., and I would like to emulate his ways. War is very, very unjust to the poor. Many people are drawn to the military because they see it as a possible way out of poverty. And so the poor get sent into these wars in unjust proportions. That was not true for Casey, but it is true for many people who enlist. In the aftermath of Hurricane Katrina there were recruiters going through the crowd in the New Orleans Astrodome trying to recruit people who had just lost everything. They were clearly trying to take advantage of people's vulnerability, to use them for the war machine, to get them into this war. In fact, I believe our deeper underlying social problem is that we think we can solve all of our problems through violence.

Adding to our misperception of how this war affects our security is the failure of our commercial media to report truthfully on the war. It fails to fulfill its responsibility to report what is really happening and often distorts or just ignores reality, rather than investigating and reporting truth. Between commercials, dominant media often repeat official views rather than challenging them. If we didn't have alternative and independent media we wouldn't know the truth about what is going on in the world. Unfortunately, however, alternative media might be preaching to the choir. The people who usually listen to it or read it are already on board with their message. Most people get their news from CNN or Fox News, which have a totally biased way of reporting. What frightens me is the thought that they could cut us off from the Internet if they ever declared martial law. At some level, I believe that New Orleans has just been practice for martial law, if they ever declare it on a wider scale—which is very frightening to consider.

If we just take fifteen extra minutes a day to educate ourselves, we would know what's truly going on in this country, what's truly going on in the world. We need to turn off the TV news and read more.

Speaking of New Orleans, the city's Mayor Ray Nagin gave a blistering interview on a local radio station, WWL-AM, in which he cried out for help and made connections between how President Bush handled Iraq and how he handled New Orleans. The mayor demanded to know why his city wasn't being helped. He exclaimed:

Well, did the tsunami victims request? Did it go through a formal process to request? . . . You know, did the Iraqi people request that we go in there? Did they ask us to go in there?
. . . We authorized $8 billion to go to Iraq lickety-quick. After 9/11, we gave the president unprecedented powers lickety-quick to take care of New York and other places. . . .

You mean to tell me that a place where you probably have thousands of people that have died and thousands more that are dying every day, that we can't figure out a way to authorize the resources that we need? Come on, man."²
What are your observations about the way New Orleans is being handled, how the media is covering it, and its relationship to the war in Iraq?

Well, I don't think the media—the mainstream media—is making connections between New Orleans and the war in Iraq, but the connections are there. The mainstream media are asking the government questions like "Where were you?," "Where was the help?" but what they're not asking is why 70 percent of the National Guard from those three Gulf states—Mississippi, Alabama, and Louisiana—are occupying Iraq and not helping out where they should be, here at home. The media should be reporting the fact that if 70 percent of our National Guardsmen and women were not in Iraq, that if most of their equipment wasn't in Iraq with them, that if funds that should have been used to reinforce the levees weren't spent bombing and occupying Iraq, that if all those things hadn't happened there would have been far less loss of life in those three Gulf states. That's what our national media should be discussing, should be debating.

The mainstream media never go deep enough to really inform people. The deeper issue here is how our resources are misused for fighting war rather than keeping the peace. The deeper issue is that the poor people of New Orleans were not abandoned after the hurricane, they were abandoned long, long ago. That's what we need to reflect on and do something about. That's what being secure really means—being secure from the unjust poverty and racism and greed that fuel the war machine.

Regarding the war in Iraq—which we're paying more than one billion dollars a day to continue—the media are also failing to say, "George Bush, you've been stating for almost three years that this war in Iraq is making America safer, but you have obviously demonstrated by this tragedy in the Gulf states that that's not true: you are making America more vulnerable."

And the people who voted for him are finally saying to themselves, "Wow, he really has made our country more vulnerable." More and more people realize that they've been duped by Bush. You can see it as Bush's approval ratings continue to sink below sea level.

And when I look at people like Donald Rumsfeld, who said that the insurgency might not be put down in Iraq for over a dozen years, I think about those soccer moms and those NASCAR dads who voted for George Bush. I think to myself, "Do they look at their kindergartners and say, 'Wow, my baby might be fighting this eternal war of aggression in Iraq, what will I do?'"

And when I *do* see pictures or news clips of National Guard troops in New Orleans, I see them with their weapons drawn and pointed at citizens. I don't see them rescuing people, I don't see them handing out food and water; I see them poised to shoot people who want food and water. I really don't think that's why people join the National Guard, I don't think that's why people join the military—to turn on their fellow citizens. I think they join to help America, not to be an enemy of regular American citizens who are struggling just to stay alive.

The issue of security is a difficult one. Bush used it to drive the country to war. When Dr. King gave his Riverside Church speech, it was at a time when the U.S. was attacking Vietnam without there really being any threat of Vietnam attacking the United States. But 9/11 was an attack on American soil. As an advocate for social change, what do you feel is the best way that we can advance peace and security at the same time?

First of all, I believe that the acts on September 11, 2001, were not acts of war, they were acts of crime. And I believe the way to deal with that is by finding the criminals and by prosecuting the crimes. That's how the Oklahoma City bombing was handled. But what we've done since 9/11 is, instead of finding the criminals and prosecuting the crimes, we've attacked, invaded, and occupied innocent countries that didn't have anything to do with it. The point is that if the U.S. only goes to find the criminals, then it cannot continue to feed the immoral war machine.

I believe 9/11 was exploited to do that—to feed the war business. George Bush says, "Oh, you can't exploit the tragedy in New Orleans and make it political." Well, what have they been doing for the past four years with 9/11? They're still trying to convince the public of connections that just don't exist. They're still trying to convince Americans that Saddam Hussein had something to do with 9/11 or that bombing Iraq is some kind of revenge for 9/11.

And I believe that if we want to make our country safer, the worst thing we can do is attack innocent countries and kill their citizens. I believe what we're doing in the Middle East is actually breeding terrorism and it's not only making our lives more vulnerable, it's putting all the pieces in place so that the lives of our children and our grandchildren will be less secure in the future.

What do we need to do? We need to get the troops out of the Middle East and Muslim countries and we need to be more fair with policies that way too heavily favor Israel. We need to stop our government from killing people and to start protecting America.

Howard Zinn, one of this country's greatest living historians, was a bombardier in World War II. At one point in his life Howard believed that there were just and unjust wars. At one point he wrote, "I enlisted in the Army Air Corps in World War II and was an eager bombardier, determined to do everything I could to help defeat fascism. Yet, at the end of the war, when I collected my little mementos—my photos, logs of some of my missions—I wrote on the folder, without really thinking, and surprising myself: 'Never Again.'"[3] Just two words, but in them is a revolution. Since writing them, Zinn has written books and articles, marched in rallies, and spoken out that there is never a just war, that the way toward creating a liberated, truly just society is to never resort to war. What are your thoughts on that?

I believe that the only reason you should use your military is to defend yourself. That would fit in with the just war theory. I can't look back on any war we've fought and say that it's just. World War I bred Hitler in World War II because our policies between the wars were so heavy-handed against the German people. I believe—and I think I'm on board with Howard Zinn about this—that if you are wise enough and you are patient enough and if you are strong enough and have enough courage, you can avoid war. Defending yourself is different from active combat and declaring war on another country. By the time we got into World War II it was pretty far gone, and they said that that was "the war to end all wars." I wish to God that that had been true. And look at every war since—we have not even declared a lot them to be wars. How many generations in this country have we damaged by our policies of aggression?

Ralph Nader, who's written a public letter of support for you,[4] also likes to raise the point that war was never declared by Congress in the current "war on terror," and that it is therefore unconstitutional. Part of President Bush's rhetoric is that this is a defensive war and that the United States has been attacked, and that when you have evidence that there are people who may be conspiring to attack, you have the right to strike them before they strike you—that's the Bush administration's preemptive doctrine.[5] If one can justify war in the name of self-defense it starts to get tricky, no?

Not tricky. Iraq was never a threat to the United States of

America. Iraq had nothing to do with the attacks on 9/11, and the person who they say is responsible for the attacks is still at large four years later. Afghanistan is in worse shape than it was before our military went in there. I've heard that the only secure place in Afghanistan is in Kabul. The drug lords are back in power; the Taliban are back in power in the provinces; they're growing more opium than they ever have before.

Iraq, by the time we attacked, was a decimated country from the years of sanctions and bombings carried out during the Clinton administration. Those sanctions and bombings killed 1.5 million people. I have heard that when our soldiers were fighting their way into Iraq, they were being challenged by Iraqi soldiers who were wearing flip-flops and using rusty weapons.

As I've said before, we're going to be paying for this mess for years with the hatred of the families in Iraq and Afghanistan that George Bush has decimated. By killing innocent South Asian and Middle Eastern people, we're making a whole lot of new enemies each day.

And, look, we're here—we don't have any ill will toward people in Iraq, and we might be the target of what George Bush's policies have created. My heart breaks for the innocent people we've been dismembering, widowing, orphaning, and killing over there. It's not just our bombs and our bullets that are killing them, it's that they don't have medicine, they don't have clean water. It's just a tragedy of immense proportions.

President Bush's policy of preemptive strikes is brutal and

wrong. It just adds to our problems. It's all to make his cronies and the other criminals in his administration even richer than they already are.

So you completely disagree with all of the rationales that the Bush administration gave for going to war?

Totally and completely.

What's your analysis?

My son was killed by Shiite insurgents. I believe George Bush created the insurgency by his failed policies and that's why my son was killed.

I think that all of the rationales the Bush administration gave were false, that George Bush is a criminal, and that he should be held accountable for what he has said and what he is doing to the world.

He said there were weapons of mass destruction, but there are none, and were none. The Downing Street memos have proven that he knew months before the invasion that Saddam Hussein didn't have weapons of mass destruction.[6]

He said that there was a link between Saddam and Al-Qaeda's terrorism. But the Downing Street memos prove that President Bush knew that there was no link. So, we had proof before, and since then we've had the 9/11 Commission confirm that Saddam had nothing to do with 9/11. We've had the Senate Intelligence

Committee report that the intelligence was absolutely false and absolutely misinterpreted; and we've had the Charles Duelfer weapons of mass destruction report say that Saddam didn't have weapons of mass destruction, and that he wouldn't have the capabilities for perhaps a decade to have such weapons.[7]

To me, you don't go in and destroy a country and let innocent young Iraqis and innocent Americans get killed because there might be a *potential* to build weapons of mass destruction at some *potential* date in the future. President Bush wants to go into every country that is thinking about getting weapons of mass destruction, but he doesn't go in and invade countries that actually have them.

In her August 29, 2005, *New York Times* article, "In the Struggle Over the Iraq War, Women Are on the Front Line," Elisabeth Bumiller writes that perhaps women feel the pain of loss more intensely than men, and that in womanhood is a certain "ferocity." I'd like to ask you about that, about the special role, if any, women have in leadership, in movement building, and the role that feminism has to offer in advancing alternative paradigms for the future—the nonviolent revolution that King advocated.

Well, I just know that as a woman and a mother who's had a child killed in this war, for me it's imperative that I do this to help my sisters. No other mother should ever go through what I'm going through—not just in this war but in future wars, future wars that they're probably thinking about and planning right now. I believe that women usually wouldn't send their own children or another mother's child to war. I believe it is our motherhood—not just our feminism, but our motherhood—that makes us such strong warriors for peace.

Do you think that the problem of aggression and war are perpetuated essentially by men, and if so, what alternatives do women offer?

I think it goes back to the motherhood thing. Men can be very nurturing, they can be very good fathers, but we women carry the babies, we love them from the minute we know they're inside of us. Mothers and the children we carry have a connection that is physical and spiritual and emotional on every level. When I think about it, my children have touched every part of me, even the inside of me. My kids were nourished inside of me for nine months and outside of me for up to eighteen months. And I've touched every part of them—even kissed their butts after they've had a bath. So I think it's a motherhood thing. Men can feel connected with children too, but I don't think it's in the same ways that mothers do.

I've seen some women who have tried to be like men in that they want to be tough; they want to show that they can be warmongers too. But I think it is anti-feminist to be a warmonger. I think we women need to always be in touch with our mother side, whether we've had children or not, and force the men of this world to protect the children—and not just our children, but the world's children.

So you don't think that there's something inherently in men that uses aggression and violence as a form of problem solving?

I don't know. I had two boys and two girls, and we raised them in a nonviolent household. And it was just such a shock to us when our son joined the military. I saw my boys be just as gentle as the girls, just as sensitive; they could cry just as easily as the girls could. In fact, my girls might have been a little tougher than the boys in that respect. I don't know if it's inherent, I don't know if it's a societal thing. I really think that, if it is something inherent, that it could be something that could be moderated. If we had strong women who were always in touch with that part of them, then I believe that we could live in a world of peace and always come from a peaceful paradigm instead of just jumping right to aggression and violence to solve things.

You mentioned just now that you were shocked when Casey said that he had joined the military. Could you speak to that—was there was a moment when you all sat around the kitchen table together and had an opportunity to talk about it as a family? Right now there are thousands of families whose children are considering enlisting but haven't yet— could you speak to those family situations?

Well, Casey was already twenty-one years old when he enlisted. He had been in college for three years. George Bush wasn't in office yet. When George Bush became his commander-in-chief, my son's doom was sealed. George Bush wanted to invade Iraq before he even ran for president. While he was still governor of Texas he was saying: "If I was commander-in-chief, this is what I would do."

Casey was promised a huge signing bonus which he never got. They promised him he could be a chaplain's assistant, which was what he really wanted to do, but, when he got to boot camp, they said that was full and he could be a Humvee mechanic or a cook. So he chose Humvee mechanic. He was promised a laptop so he could take classes from wherever he was deployed in the world. He never got that. He was promised that he would never see combat and then he was killed five days after he landed in Iraq.

Casey joined before 9/11. His recruiter lied to him and said, "Even if there's a war, you won't see combat." And they are still telling our children that. They're telling the children that they won't have to go to Iraq if they sign up. You know, there's a contract that is signed between the recruiter and the recruit, and it's only binding on the recruit, not the recruiter.

By the time Casey had joined, it was too late. He didn't talk to us before he did it. He signed on the dotted line and he took the oath of service and then he came home and told us. We were devastated.

For any of our children to be killed in war is unspeakable. We never even spanked the kids. We never solved problems with violence in our house. I used to promise the kids, even the girls, that I would never, ever let them go off to a war. And I broke that promise with Casey.

To families who may be in similar situations I would say that as long as we have leadership that uses our children so recklessly and so callously, do not let them sign up for the military. There are so many alternatives. You can contact the Central Committee for Conscientious Objectors or the American Friends Service Committee. Please, please, don't let your kids be recruited. I would rather see my kids not get a military-financed college education than see them be misused and abused by the leadership of this country.

Karen Houppert's article in the September 12, 2005, issue of *The Nation* is called "Military Recruiters Are Now Targeting Sixth Graders: Who's Next?" In it, she writes "The Army has increased its recruitment campaign budget by $500 million this year, and it is slated to introduce a new ad campaign in September emphasizing patriotism. . . . On the sly, recruiters have helped high schoolers cheat on entrance exams, fudge their drug tests and hide police records, as the *New York Times* reported in May. The *Times* exposé revealed that "the Army investigated 1,118 'recruiting improprieties' last year ranging from coercing young people to lying to them. It substantiated 320 of these." You've mentioned that the military lied to Casey, that they made promises to get him to join but then never delivered. As a way of putting it out there for other families who may be vulnerable to recruitment, could you speak a little about what Casey may have wanted to gain by joining?

Well, Casey always wanted to serve people—his friends, his family, his church, his community, his country. So I'm sure that went into his decision-making. He thought he would be serving America. He thought he would be protecting his country. I didn't know that the wars we wage are rarely to defend the United States of America, so I didn't teach him that.

From the time we are born we are taught to be loyal to symbols and we're instilled with this false sense of patriotism. Instead of being loyal to a sense of community, to cooperation, to what a true democracy would look like, we're loyal to a flag, to an Uncle Sam. People think that we have to be loyal to the president even when he is disloyal to his office and betrays the country. I believe that true patriots love their country but know that it can always be better; so they work and are willing to sacrifice everything, like my family has.

The recruiters, I would say, in the majority of cases patently lie to young people in order recruit them. The recruiters are operating on a quota system. They're under tremendous pressure to make their quotas because, in a sense, their lives are on the line: recruiters who want to give up and move on to another job specialty within the military are told if they do that, they'll be shipped off to Iraq.

Then there are the retention rates in Iraq. The military are touting those, but they're not telling people that—and I've heard this from many, many soldiers in Iraq— they're telling soldiers that if they reenlist then they'll get a "signing bonus,"a reenlistment bonus, and that if they don't reenlist, then they're going to be subject to "Stop Loss," which means that they're going to have to stay in the country anyway.[8]

"Stop Loss"—President Bush instituted that, I believe, around October or November 2003. And the kids think that when they sign up for four years that they're actually going to get out in four years. But that's not how it goes. There's little fine print that says you have four more years of "Ready Reserve." This means that new recruits can be "stop loss-ed" after their four years and made to stay another four years or until they're not needed anymore. And so the kids are like, "Wow, we signed up for four years, we've been to Iraq two or three times already, and you're telling us we can't get out? We've served our country, let us out!" This is what I'm hearing from these kids in Iraq.

People say, "Oh, they're not kids, they're adults." I'm sorry, but an eighteen- or nineteen-year-old is not an adult. My son was twenty-four when they killed him. He was single, no children. You know, by twenty-four I was already married with three children. A person of eighteen and nineteen years old is vulnerable. They don't know about life yet. They don't know what they're getting into. And so these kids in Iraq are e-mailing me and they're saying, "We are being held hostage here; we cannot come home."

And they're saying, "You and the peace movement are the only hope—the ones who are saying 'bring our troops home now' are our only hope of getting out of here!"

One young man e-mailed me, saying, "I feel like someone who has been convicted of a crime that I didn't commit, but I cannot get out of prison."

So that's what they're doing. I equate recruiters with used car salesmen—they'll say anything to get you to sign on the dotted line. But once you do, you're screwed. If the car falls apart, that's too bad, and if you're lied to by your government, that's too bad too.

Did Casey ever receive the funds he was promised?

The recruiters promised him $20,000. When he finished boot camp they gave him $4,000, and they said the rest of it would go toward his education. As I mentioned earlier, they also promised he could be a chaplain's assistant, but that never happened either. He had to be a mechanic. And, like I said, they never let him take a class and they killed him before he could claim that benefit.

Could you describe a little about your arc from being a mother—who comes from neither a military nor an activist background—to the woman who's on her way to Washington, D.C., to lead a rally demanding that the President of the United States end his war and occupation of Iraq?

Well, after Casey was killed, my whole family knew he died for nothing. It was senseless and needless.

I guess I wasn't an activist, but I've always been a champion for people who are voiceless. I was a youth minister for eight years and, let me tell you, I was always bumping heads with the church's adult leadership. I was always trying to make our church a more welcoming and responsive place for people. I was the youth minister, so I wanted the youth to feel welcome and part of the church community. I was always doing that, whether we had a supportive priest or an unsupportive priest. I was always making sure that the people who I was in charge of were being treated respectfully. And I have always done that with my children, too. I believed that it doesn't matter how old a human being you are, you deserve to receive respect. That's how I raised my children. If they were having problems, we would always try to work it out so that they would be in charge of their own problems, but we would help them in any way that we could. But if a mother's child is hurt, then the mother becomes something fierce. And when my son was killed, I became something fierce.

It's a horrific thing that happens to a parent when his or her child is killed or dies from any cause before the parents. When you have to bury a child, it's disordered, it's not natural. And when you arrive at the moment that you learn that your child is dead, that's the point where you pray for death yourself. But I didn't die. There's some reason that God kept me alive. And there's some reason why Casey was taken from us. We had to make sense out of that because it was so senseless.

One day about three weeks after Casey was killed, my daughter came in and said, "Mom, do you want to hear a poem I wrote?" And I said, "Well, of course I do," because she never shared a poem with me before or since. But when she shared her poem with me, that gave me a reason for living and really saved my life. I'm not going to recite it, but it's called "A Nation Rocked to Sleep." The last part of it says:

Have you ever heard the sound of a nation being rocked to sleep?
The leaders want to keep you numb so the pain won't be too deep,
But if we the people let them continue, another mother will weep.
Have you ever heard the sound of a nation rocked to sleep?[9]

And at that moment I knew that I had to do everything I could to bring our kids home so not one mother would have to go through what I'm going through.

There are thousands of mothers in this country who have gotten that knock on the door, and I feel responsible for every single one of them.[10] Every day there are more. My heart breaks for every single one of them. So I started. I started writing. I started asking questions.

People think I just fell off a pumpkin truck in Crawford on August 6, 2005, and started asking the President these questions. But I've been doing it almost ever since Casey died. I didn't do it before Casey died because I didn't think one person could make a difference. After Casey died I thought, well, if I can't make a difference, at least I can go to my grave knowing I tried. But I've since learned that everything we do makes a difference.

The action on August 6, 2005, was the culmination of months of work, of working my butt off. You know, this isn't new to me, traveling from city to city, being on a different form of transportation every day to go from one place to the next. It's something I've been doing for a long time now.

On August 3, 2004, fourteen marines were killed in one incident and it was reported as an "Oh, by the way" thing on CNN. It was rare for me to be home watching TV, because I never watch TV and I'm never home—but there I was, home and watching the tube, when I saw George Bush speaking at some luncheon. He had just started another vacation in Crawford. He didn't mention the incident, he didn't mention the fourteen marines, but he did say that what we're doing in Iraq is a good thing and that all of the soldiers, marines, sailors, airpersons who have died have died for a noble cause.

That got me upset right away, because I don't believe a war of aggression against a country that is no threat to the United States is a noble cause. I don't believe guarding oil fields that belong to another country is a noble cause worth dying for. I don't believe that the war machine feeding off of our young people's flesh and blood is a noble cause. And I have never believed it, even before the lead-up to the war—the insane rush to the war.

Then President Bush said something that has always infuriated me. He said, "We have to complete the mission to honor the sacrifices of the ones who have fallen." For months I had been asking, just because Casey was killed, why would I want one more person killed? Why would I want one more mother, Iraqi or American, to go through what I am going through? Why would I want one more family to be torn apart, just because my son was killed?

I believe it is immoral to continue this war, to say we have to kill more people—we've already killed so many people.

After my son had been killed I felt like a failure because I had been working so hard and it didn't seem like anything was being accomplished. I am the type of person who gives my heart and my soul 100 percent to something—but I was used to seeing results. So there I was with my broken heart, typing an e-mail out of frustration and grief. I was literally typing as I was thinking— I was writing to my e-mail list—that I was going to Dallas to the Veterans for Peace convention, and that when I was finished there, I was going down to Crawford to confront that motherf— er and make him answer some questions. First and foremost, what noble cause did my son die for? And I promised myself that I was going to demand that he quit using my son's honorable name and my family's sacrifice to justify the continued killing.

At that point, I thought it was just me and my sister going to Crawford. But as soon as I hit send on that e-mail I immediately started getting responses. The Veterans for Peace responded and asked, "How can we help you?" The Crawford Peace House—I didn't even know that it existed—wrote me asking how they could help me. And by the time we finally went to Crawford on a Saturday morning, there were already over a hundred people who showed up with us.

How many people did you send that e-mail to?

Probably about three hundred. As soon as I did I started getting so many responses back from people because everybody was forwarding the email around. Then I thought, "Well, if I did this I might as well send out an e-mail to media contacts too." And by the time we got there, there were probably about fifty media there and about 125 people going up to the march with us.

But when President Bush wouldn't meet with me, I just sat down and said, "OK, I'm not moving. I'm not moving until he comes out and meets with me. And if he doesn't come out, I'll sit here until he leaves for his vacation." And then, oh my God, it just snowballed. Actually, I don't want to say "snowballed" because it was so hot! People have said that we were a spark that lit a prairie fire, and prairie fires spread really fast. We had six people stay with us that night and we had twenty-five the next night and fifty the next night, and then by the time Thursday came, we had seven hundred.

Ann Wright, my Camp Casey comandante, kept really good track of everybody. And then, well, you know the media response just made the prairie fire spread faster and further. You know why? Because the movement was already there. At that point, more than half the country knew that this war was a huge mistake and believed that our troops should be coming home. You see it in the polls.[11] And that's a majority of Americans. That's millions of Americans who believe that. So the movement is there. I think we just needed somewhere to focus our energy, and Camp Casey turned out to be such a place of love and acceptance and peace. It was the right thing for us to do, and it was the right time and place.

Could we go back to the moment when your daughter read you her poem? That's seems to be the moment when you passed through the flame and came out a person transformed. I'd like to hear you comment on that moment a little more and then the next steps you took from that moment forward. Did you feel that something had changed inside you?

I think the only thing that really changed was my feeling that, like I said, even if I couldn't change anything, at least I would know that I had tried to prevent more needless deaths. And one of the first steps I took after Carly read me her poem was to join Military Families Speak Out.

I had already been in contact with the father of a family whose son was killed in the same incident Casey had been killed in. This man and I had come to the same conclusion, we had reached the same place politically—that this war was a massive mistake, a war based on lies—but he had been an activist before his son was killed, marching in rallies and stuff like that. So he founded an organization called Military Families Speak Out and I joined it. I sent the organization a letter and I also sent them my daughter Carly's poem, and they posted it on their website.

On July 4, 2004, there was a speaking opportunity in Berkeley, California. Since I live close to Berkeley I said, "Well, you know what, I'm not ready to speak yet, but I will go and support whoever speaks." My friend Bill Mitchell went, and another lady that I didn't know yet named Jane Bright went too, and we met each other. I ended up speaking and I really haven't stopped since that day, the Fourth of July 2004.

I also got involved in another organization called realvoices.org. My daughter Carly and I recorded some commercials. My commercial was picked up by MoveOn.org and was played in swing states. I did a lot of campaigning in "red" states—not for Kerry but *against* George Bush.

Then in December 2004 I had a brainstorm. When certain ideas just come to me like that I feel very inspired, they come out of the blue, like I'm not even thinking them myself. What was the brainstorm? To start an organization comprised of people who have had their loved ones killed in Iraq: Gold Star Families for Peace. So I got together with Jane and Bill and my sister Dede, and we formed the nucleus of the group and formally went as an organization in January 2005 trying to meet with Donald Rumsfeld. And ever since I formed Gold Star Families for Peace I have been out on the road speaking in rallies, doing interviews, writing, resisting.

People always ask, "So what did you do before your son was killed?" I say, "I was a mom and I worked at jobs." Then they ask, "Yeah, well, did you write?" No. "Did you speak?" No. You know, I think that I just opened my heart and my soul and let whatever needed to come out, come out. And that's what has had a huge effect. I speak and I just trust that whatever I need to say is said and that it will affect people.

I've heard you mention Henry David Thoreau and Ralph Waldo Emerson as inspirations. Could you comment on them and who else inspires your work?

I have only really touched on Ralph Waldo in respect to his meeting with Henry David. I call them RW and HD. Henry David Thoreau inspires me several ways. He said that "You don't own your possessions, they own you" and "Simplify, simplify, simplify." It's really hard in America to be a non-consumer or to not want to have many possessions. But now that I've been on the road for a few months, I've basically cut my life down to a suitcase. I leave one suitcase at home and have one suitcase that I bring with me. It really makes your life a lot easier. But all that kind of changed at Camp Casey since I accumulated about ten big boxes of things that thoughtful people mailed to me from all over the country.

Another thing about Henry David Thoreau that inspires me is that he refused to pay his poll tax. He detested slavery and the U.S. war against Mexico and preferred to go to jail than to have his taxes pay for killing and enslaving people. So they arrested him and he went to jail. But somebody paid his taxes for him, which enraged him, and he was released from prison.

It also inspires me to think of when his friend Ralph Waldo came to visit him and said something like, "Henry, what are you doing in there?" Henry David answered, "Ralph Waldo, what are you doing out there?" For Thoreau, so long as slavery existed and was legal, and the U.S. was invading Mexico, jail was the only place for a moral person to be.

Like back in Thoreau's time, I really believe that what this country is doing now is so corrupt, dishonest, and immoral that a truly civic-minded person should disobey. We have the right to break immoral laws and risk going to jail for that. That's what Thoreau did and what he wrote about. It's inspiring.

Other people who inspire me are, of course, Martin Luther King, Jr., and Gandhi. But the biggest inspiration in my whole life is my son Casey, who didn't want to go to war but thought it was his commitment; he felt it was his duty, felt he had to be there to support his buddies. He didn't want to go to the battle that he was killed in, he was terribly afraid, but he went anyway to save the lives of his buddies. I think that my son is a martyr for peace and his death will count for peace, and I will spend my last penny and my last breath making sure that happens.

And along the way you are you willing to get arrested doing civil disobedience?

Yeah, me and a lot of other people all across the country. People like Camilo Mejía, who refused to go back to Iraq, and Kevin Benderman ,who refused to go to Iraq, both of whom were arrested and put in jail. They too believe that being in prison is better than killing innocent people and being involved in immoral things.

On February 15, 2003, millions of people around the world took to the streets to protest the looming war against Iraq. From Barcelona, where they banged pots and pans in resistance, to New York, where protesters clashed with police, people organized and demonstrated. Two days later the *New York Times* ran a remarkable cover article by Patrick E.

Tyler called "A New Power in the Streets." The article began with these words:

> The fracturing of the Western Alliance over Iraq and the huge antiwar demonstrations around the world this weekend are reminders that there may still be two superpowers on the planet: the United States and world opinion. . . . President Bush appears to be eyeball to eyeball with a tenacious new adversary: millions of people who flooded the streets of New York and dozens of other world cities to say they are against war based on the evidence at hand.

Thoughts?

We, the People, really are a superpower, and George W. Bush is our employee.

Do you believe that taking to the streets makes a difference?

Yes, I believe it does, but also so does sitting in a ditch.[12]

I'd like to ask a question about the issue of movements and leaders. You are credited with reenergizing and re-mobilizing the antiwar movement. Your leadership is bringing people together to speak out and to focus pressure on the Bush administration to change course. President Bush hasn't met with you a second time, as you're demanding, but he's been forced to respond to your questions. In this moment

that we're in, how would you, through your observations and experiences, comment on the relationship between movements and leaders?

That's a hard question. First of all, I don't think that Bush really responded to my questions. He responded to my presence in Crawford and answered questions I hadn't asked him yet. Maybe a movement needs a leader. Maybe it needs someone to focus on. Like I said before, I never wanted to be a leader of a movement, I just want our kids to come home from Iraq.

Being a leader—sometimes I lay awake at night with the responsibility of it. Not just the people who tear me down and lie about me and mischaracterize me or twist what I say—that doesn't bother me nearly as much as all the people who are counting on me. And that reminds me that I have a big responsibility. I don't think everything I do or say should be scrutinized so carefully. You know, they don't scrutinize everything George Bush says or does. They don't scrutinize *anything* he says or does. But they scrutinize what I say and do very carefully, and I'm just a mom who wants the war to be over.

I'm not perfect and I never claimed I was perfect, and I never claim to speak for 100 percent of the American public. So it's a lot of responsibility I didn't exactly ask for. But I didn't ask for Casey to be killed either. I was talking to my oldest daughter, Carly, and I said for some reason that our family was called to make some terrible sacrifices to make this country a better place and to make the world a better place. Just being the people we are, I think we must be a very special family to be asked to do so much.

What did you want to say to President Bush when you were camped outside his place in Crawford, Texas?

Well, of course the first thing I wanted to ask was: "What noble cause did Casey die for? Was it freedom and democracy?" *Bullshit.* He died for oil. He died to make Bush's friends richer. He died to expand American imperialism in the Middle East. We're not freer here, thanks to Bush's USA PATRIOT Act. Iraq is not free. What do I want to say? "Bush, you get America out of Iraq. You need to start respecting the people of the United States and the world, which will do more to affect terrorism, to make the world a safer place to live." That's what I want to say. And there, I used the "I" word—imperialism. And now I'm going to use another "I" word—impeachment—because we cannot have these people pardoned. They need to be tried for war crimes and sent to jail.

In Crawford, Bush didn't come out to meet you, didn't answer your questions . . .

I figured out that he couldn't come and talk to me because there is no noble cause. He didn't have an answer, so he couldn't come out. He couldn't answer saying "freedom and democracy" because the new Iraqi constitution and the Iraqi government—they're not working. I challenged him, I said, "You don't spread freedom and democracy by forcing it on a people and by killing them." And he was saying that we are there "to make America safer." Well, it's very obvious that he's making America more vulnerable by what he's doing in Iraq, so he can't say that anymore.

Then, two weeks ago today, August 29, 2005, on the Monday of Hurricane Katrina, he finally said what was probably the first truthful thing he has said his whole life: he said that we're there to protect the oil fields from terrorists. And so, even if I had a meeting with him I wasn't going to let him lie to me. I didn't think he would tell me the truth, but I was going to let him know I knew he was lying. Just like when he sent Deputy Chief of Staff Joe Hagen and National Security Advisor Stephen J. Hadley to come out to meet with me. I told them, "You guys are lying to me. And don't make the mistake that just because I'm a grieving mother that I'm stupid. Because I'm not stupid. I'm very well informed. And I don't even believe you believe what you're telling me." That's how I talked to them and that's how I would have talked to President Bush. They said, "We didn't come out here thinking we'd change your mind on policy." And I said, "Yes, you did." They thought they were going to intimidate me, that they were going to impress me with the high level of administration official they had sent out, but they didn't.

Prior to Camp Casey you had actually met once with President Bush.

I met with the president in June 2004, a couple of months after Casey was killed. We were summoned to Fort Irwin in

Washington State to have a sit-down with the President. My entire family went. When I met him, I met a man who had no compassion in him. He had no heart. He doesn't care at all about us. We tried to show him pictures of Casey. He wouldn't look at them. He wouldn't even acknowledge Casey's name. He called me "Mom" throughout the entire meeting. He acted like we were at a tea party, like it was something fun, that we should just be so pleased that we got to meet with the president who killed our son.

What else did he say?

He said, "So who are we honoring here?" He didn't even know Casey's name. Somebody should have whispered to him, "Mr. President, this is the Sheehan family, their son Casey was killed in Iraq." We thought that was pretty disrespectful to not even know Casey's name and to walk in and say, "So who are we honorin' here?" Like, "Let's get on with it, let's get somebody honored here."

Did the two of you talk?

The first thing he said to me was "Mom, I can't imagine your loss. I can't imagine losing a loved one, you know, whether it be a mother, a father, a sister or brother." And I stopped him, and I said, "You have two children. Try to imagine *them* being killed in a war. *How would that make you feel?*" I don't think he was expecting that, and I think I saw a little bit of human flicker in his eye, like he might have connected for a moment, because this is a man that's disconnected from humanity. Then I said, "Trust me, you don't want to go there." And you know what he told me? He goes, "You're right, I don't." And so I said, "Well, thank you for putting me there," and he moved on to the next person.

A little while later we were talking, and he went up to my oldest daughter and said, "So who are you to the loved one?" And Carly goes, "Casey was my brother." And George Bush says, "I wish I could bring your loved one back, to fill the hole in your heart." And Carly said, "Yeah, so do we." And Bush said, "I'm sure you do," and he gave her the dirtiest look and turned his back on her and ignored her for the rest of the meeting. And then a little later on in the meeting, I said, "Why were we invited here? We didn't vote for you in 2000, and we're certainly not going to vote for you in 2004." And he said, "It's not about politics," which is just baloney.

Everybody else I've talked to who has met with him has had about the same experiences that my family and I did. He comes in and says something like "I want to extend the gratitude of the nation and express my condolences," but as he says it his eyes don't convey a sense he means it. He's just talking. We left our meeting with him feeling worse than when we walked in. We left our meeting with the president feeling even more determined to stop the madness in Iraq.

You have said "Rep. Walter Jones (R-NC) has realized that he had been duped into supporting the invasion." Have any public officials

expressed support for your activities? How about international leaders?

No world leaders,[13] but I have heard from many members of Congress, including Frank Pallone, Jr., who we're on our way right now to meet in Westfield, New Jersey, where he's organized an outdoor press conference about Iraq.[14]

President Bush has said that the antiwar movement is weakening the United States and emboldening terrorists. Comments?

That's an old Vietnam argument. I believe his preemptive policy and war of aggression on countries that are no threat to the United States weakens America. It's obvious that what he's doing is emboldening terrorists and it's recruiting terrorists. I want to say: "Prove it. Show me where anything we're doing is emboldening the terrorists."

Mark Danner's article in yesterday's *New York Times Magazine* describes how Americans in Iraq are "increasingly irrelevant" to a situation that has deteriorated beyond U.S. control.[15] How do you respond to President Bush saying that we should "stay the course"?

I respond, "How can you stay a course that is so obviously not working? Turn around, you're going the wrong way." He has betrayed us, and, by telling us that everything is going well in Iraq, he's still betraying us. It's truly criminal.

But it is our right and responsibility as Americans to speak out and challenge our government when our government is wrong. I'm not one of the immature patriots who says ,"I stand proud by my country, right or wrong." Our country is wrong now—the policies of our country are responsible for killing tens of thousands of innocent people, detaining unknown thousands of people, occupying places that do not belong to us, and I won't stand by and let that happen anymore. I believe that if anybody tries to tell us that we don't have the civic right to speak out, organize, inform one another, and resist, then they are the ones who are unpatriotic, they're un-American, and their attacks are not going to stop us.

Speaking of attacks, did the Bush administration, his Secret Service people, or anyone else hassle you while you were camped out at Crawford, Texas?

There were threats of arrest, but no one on our side was ever arrested. The Secret Service tried to intimidate us the first day by saying that if we stayed, we would probably be run over.

How do you respond to the other parents of service people who say protests dishonor their son or daughter who served?

I respect the way they feel. They have the same loss that I have. Our children came home in flag-draped coffins. But I respectfully disagree with them. I believe that this war is based on lies and all of our children are dead for no reason. I want to make meaning out of my son's death—and all of their deaths—by making them count for nonviolence and for bringing the troops home. They can protest any way they want. If that's the way they have to grieve and get over their losses, then I respect that because I know how painful it is just to live your life after losing a child. And if these people need to get over their grief this way, I want them to have the space they need to express themselves as they will, and I would hope that they would give me the same space.

Movements like the present antiwar movement are sometimes criticized as being reactionary, defined primarily by what they are against. We touched on it earlier, but I want to ask you directly: what are you for?

I'm for a world that solves its grievances by peaceful means and diplomacy and not by force. I'm for a country that doesn't use its young people as cannon fodder and bullet sponges to kill innocent people and to die for no reason. And I'm for peace. I'm for peaceful resolution to problems and not violent resolutions.

Since joining the peace movement you've met so many different people and you've heard so many different stories. I'd like to ask you to share a story or an incident that changed you since taking this path.

During the first Saturday that we were at Camp Casey we had had an amazing rally, and the following day we had hundreds of people come out to join us for a nice prayer service, but that's when a man shot a gun off at us. Not directly at us—he was on his property, and we heard it blast during our prayer service. So, I was real busy, I was real tired, I was having doubts about what I was doing. And this man came up to me, and I could tell he was a soldier even though he was in civilian clothes. And I was thinking, "Uh-oh, this doesn't look good." But he sat down and he said, "Ma'am, I wanted to come here because I have something for you." He said, "I was in the First Cavalry. I'm retired now and I work out at Fort Hood as a civilian. But I have something for you." And he handed me a painted rock that had the First Cavalry symbol on it—because my son was First Cav' too. And he brought three pictures of his buddies who were killed in Iraq. And he sat down and he said, "I honor what you're doing. And I just want to tell you that the majority of people who are in the military honor what you're doing. Even if we don't all agree with you—but most of us do agree with you—what you are doing is absolutely right and you have to keep doing it for us." That just gave me a lot of encouragement and a lot of strength to keep on doing what I'm doing.

I think what moves me most are the stories of the people who have been affected by this war, the Iraqi people who e-mail me and thank me for what I'm doing—the Iraqi people who tell me that what we're saying is correct. It's not just me that's saying that the Iraqi people don't need our help—they tell me that they don't need our help. They say, "We are the cradle of civilization. We were a civilization, we were doing math and engineering, and you guys in Europe didn't even have the written word. We can rebuild our own country. We don't need your help. We don't need your money. We've been through serious problems before. Just get out."

So I hear from Iraqi people who thank us for what we're doing in the peace movement. I know there are some parents of killed soldiers who don't agree with me, but I hear from so many who do. I hear from parents who have children over there who thank me for doing what we're doing. And I hear from Iraq vets who have joined me in this struggle—and Jeff Key here is one of them—who say that what we're doing over there is absolutely immoral and it's dehumanizing and it needs to come to an end. Those are the stories of people that I treasure the most. I appreciate all the millions of Americans who have supported us who don't have skin in the game, like we have. And whenever I hear another one of those stories or hear a family who's been devastated by this gratuitous war, it just gives me more strength to work harder to try and prevent the tragedies.

Many of the people who are reading these words right now aren't able to go to Washington for the big demonstrations. What is your message to them?

First, we all need to speak to our employee, the President of the United States. As his employers, he needs to speak with us as often as possible with as many of us as he can. The will of the people is greater than the presidency. And when the people speak out, it's the president's responsibility to listen. He is there to serve us, not the other way around. He tries to insulate himself from dissension or opposing viewpoints, and that's one of his major problems.

This isn't about politics. It's about what is good for America and what's best for our security and how far this president has taken us away from both.

Second, everybody needs to work for peace. There are a lot of us working our butts off for it, but we need more. If everybody did a little something every day, it wouldn't take much time, you know, something very easy. Just send a letter to your congressman to say bring the troops home, and that we'll support you if you support peace, and if you don't support peace we'll withdraw our support of you.

Third, talk to young people who are thinking of going into the military. Get them to see another point of view, give them options aside from going into the military. Show them the facts and the possibilities.

Research. Communicate. Resist. Inform yourself about what's going on in the world and talk with others. Stand with us.

I also want to say this: thank you, America, for the love and support that you sent to all of us at Camp Casey and that we're still receiving. And thank you, America, for giving me back my hope—my hope for our country and my hope for my life.

September 12, 2005

TWO

Comments in Westfield, New Jersey

Cindy Sheehan's comments at
Congressman Frank Pallone's press conference
on the lawn of the East Broad Street Municipal Building

LIKE CONGRESSMAN PALLONE SAID, I WENT TO Camp Casey because we need to hold somebody accountable for the tragedy and the travesty going on in Iraq. I thought that my family was alone. I thought nobody in America cared about what was going on in Iraq. I thought nobody cared about the losses that our country was sustaining—not only the ones who have been killed, but the ones who have been terribly wounded, and the ones who are coming home maybe not physically wounded, but mentally wounded. I have friends in my organization, Gold Star Families for Peace, whose son was home from Iraq for months before they found him hanging by a garden hose in their basement. He couldn't get the help he needed from the Veterans Administration. This war is taking a terrible,

terrible toll on our country and our human resources and our treasury. But who is asking the president the hard questions?

When reports came out showing that there were no weapons of mass destruction, nobody asked him: "What are we still doing there? Why are our children still dying? Why are innocent Iraqis still dying?"

When it started coming out that there is no link between Saddam Hussein and 9/11, nobody asked: "Why are our troops still there? Why are our young people still dying? Why are innocent Iraqis still dying?"

When the Downing Street memos came out that proved, categorically, that the Bush administration knew months before the invasion that that there were no weapons of mass destruction, knew that there was no link between Saddam Hussein and 9/11, nobody asked them: "Why are our troops still there? Why is everybody still dying? Why are you spending billions of our hard earned tax dollars to continue this blunder of a war?"

Millions of people are standing behind what we did at Camp Casey. Congressman Pallone was one of the first to contact me in support of what we're doing—working together to bring our troops home. We need to say to the Bush government: "Bring our troops home immediately." The people who are running our country don't seem to plan on ever bringing our troops home.

Instead of dismantling our bases over there, they're building new ones, some the size of Sacramento, California, and the Iraqi people see that. Our military presence there is fueling—

not extinguishing—the insurgency that's killing Iraqis and killing Americans.

I want to thank Congressman Pallone for inviting me here today. I know that he, the Camp Casey movement, and all the organizations that support me will have a long association to build peace in this country.

Congressman Pallone and we know that this is a war that never should have happened. Not one of our innocent American soldiers should be dead, and no one else should be dying. We need to ask the president: "Why are our young people still there? Why are you fuelling the insurgency? Why are your policies making America less safe? When are you going to bring our troops home?"

Thank you.

September 12, 2005

THREE

Speech at the D.C. Protest

*Edited transcript of Cindy Sheehan's speech
at the United for Peace and Justice rally, Washington, D.C.*

AHHHH, I LOVE THE SMELL OF PATRIOTIC DISSENT
in the afternoon.

As we stand here on the grounds of a monument that is dedicated, to the father of our country, George Washington, we are
reminded that he is well known for apocryphal stories of never
being able to tell a lie. I find it so ironic that there is another man
here named George who stays in this town between vacations,
and who never seems to be able to tell the truth. It is tragic for us
that our bookend presidents named George have two completely different relationships with honesty.

I also find it ironic and heartbreaking that my son, Casey,
who was a brave person, tall and proud, who loved his country
and was honest beyond measure, could be sent to his death by

someone who is even too cowardly to meet with a broken-hearted mom, let alone go and fight, like Casey did, in the illegal and immoral war of his generation.

We are losing our best and our brightest in a country that was never a threat to the United States of America: Iraq was and still is no danger to our security or to "our way of life." The weapons of mass destruction and mass deception reside in this town: they are the neocons who pull the strings and the members of Congress who have spent with reckless abandon, practically giving George and company a blank check to run our country into monetary and moral bankruptcy. We are out here in force today to take our country back, and to restore true democracy and sanity to our political process. The time is now and we are here because we love our country and we won't let the reckless maniacs destroy her any further.

We, as a young colony of Great Britain, broke from another tyrant, King George the Third. Well, I wish our George the Third were here today to see us out here in force protesting against his war and against his murderous policies. The president is not here, though, because he is out gallivanting around the country somewhere pretending that he cares about the people who are in the path of Hurricane Rita. We know that the president cares nothing for the people of America: Katrina[1], Iraq, and his idiotic response to 9/11 are evidence of that.

George Bush, we are here today to tell you that we are a majority and we will not rest until you bring our young people home from the Middle East, and not until you start putting money into rebuilding our communities: the ones natural disasters destroy, and the ones that your callous and racist war economy are decimating. We won't allow you to take any more money out of social programs to finance Halliburton in rebuilding the Gulf States.

Our bank account is empty. George, this is our rainy day and you have failed us miserably. Stop pouring money into the pockets of the war profiteers and into building permanent bases in Iraq. It is time to bring our billions of dollars home from Iraq too!

The Camp Casey movement that hunkered down in Crawford, Texas, this past August taught us that we the people of America have the power, and we can and should name our national policy and make sure it is carried out.

I constantly get asked if we are making a difference and if we think that we will actually stop the war. Well, looking back at how Vietnam was ended, and looking back at the history of our country, most notably in the women's suffrage, labor, and civil rights movements, *we the people* are the only ones who have been able to transform history and affect true and lasting change here in America. So to those people who question if we are making a difference: I say go back to school and read your history books!

We are here to tell the media, Congress, and this criminal and criminally negligent administration: *We are not going away!*

We in the peace movement need to agree on one thing: yes, the U.S. needs an exit plan from Iraq, but it is not a *suggestion*, it is a *command*. Our command to the government is: have all of our military personnel and paid killer mercenaries out of Iraq within six months. Have the generals carry out the command. Simple. It's not brain surgery, and I think it is so easy even President Bush can sign the order. We can't give his administration any wiggle room or long-term strategy sessions. For one thing, when our leaders "strategize," we are put in even more jeopardy; they have proven that they are not too bright and not even a little bit compassionate. But the most important thing is that people are dying every day in Iraq for absolutely no reason except lies.

We have to say *now* because the people in our government are saying *never*.

We can't compromise, we can't say please, and we can't retreat. If we do, our country is doomed.

We have to honor the sacrifices of our loved ones by completing the mission of peace and justice. It is time.

Bring our troops home *now*!

September 24, 2005

FOUR

Warhawk Republicans and Antiwar Democrats: What's the Difference?

I SPENT THE PAST WEEK IN WASHINGTON, D.C., visiting many offices of our elected officials: Senators, congresspersons—pro-war and antiwar, Democrat and Republican. With a few notable exceptions, all our employees toed party lines.

I thank those who met with me, because—except for Senator Barbara Boxer (D-CA)—I was not one of their constituents. I believe that the Republicans who did meet with me, whether they knew it or not, were breaking with their leader on this, since he was too cowardly to meet with me.

The Warhawks I met made my skin crawl. They are supporting a war that is so obviously neither in our nation's best interest nor making us more secure. I heard from Senators

Elizabeth Dole (R-NC) and John McCain (R-AZ) and Representative Marilyn Musgrave (R-CO) about 9/11 and "fighting them over there, so we don't have to fight them over there." That made me sick. The Bush administration exploited 9/11, and our national anxiety about possible future attacks, in order to invade a country that had nothing to do with the attacks on our country. Now, in the aftermath of those lies, tens of thousands of innocent Iraqi civilians are dead, along with 2,000 of our brave young men and women. What makes Iraqi babies and families less precious than ours? The only crime that the Iraqi people committed was being born in the wrong place at the wrong time. George took his war of terror to their doorsteps. I even asked Senator Dole when she thought the occupation would be able to end and she was incredulous that I would even think of Iraq as an occupation: she sees it as a liberation. I really wanted to know how many of them we have to kill before she considers that they were liberated.

The Warhawks—or warniks, as I like to call them—also use the rationale that Saddam Hussein used weapons of mass destruction against his own people. I asked Senator Dole three times where Saddam got those weapons, but she wouldn't answer me. Because the smiling, kind, patronizing Warhawkette knew where Saddam got the weapons: He got them from the U.S.A. Saddam was a bad guy, but he was our bad guy (see the famous picture of the grinning Rummy shaking Hussein's hand)[1] until he decided to sell his oil to Russia and France for euros . . . then the official position became "Oh my gosh, Saddam kills his own people!"

We didn't care about Saddam killing his own people after the first Gulf War when President Bush I encouraged the people of Iraq to rise up against Saddam. We didn't care about the Iraqi children dying off during the Clinton years as a result of the devastating sanctions. In March 2003 those things suddenly became so urgently important to current President Bush that he ordered our troops to invade and occupy Iraq. The memo to Congress where George asks for the authority to invade Iraq specifically mentions weapons of mass destruction and terrorism. It says nothing about Saddam being a "bad guy" or about spreading "freedom and democracy" to Iraq. The reasons for our continued occupation change as fast as the old reasons are proven to be lies.

It was horrible to talk to these three warmongering Republicans. I almost felt like I had to take a shower after each visit. But they did not affect my resolve. Representative Musgrave was openly hostile when we were ushered (by her very nice staff) into her office. Ms. Musgrave actually has a son in the service, but she got very defensive when I asked which branch of the service her son, who is stationed in Italy, is in. I was asking mother to mother, but she basically said it wasn't any of my business. I told her she must be very worried about her son and that he would be in my prayers.

I know that it is hard to have a child in military service, whether in Iraq or Italy. She "supports the President" 100 percent. Do these politicians not realize that the people are withdrawing their support for this war and for this president at an unprecedented clip? To support President Bush at this point is to support a sinking stone. To support him and Dick Cheney at any time is a tragic mistake of immense proportions.

The Warwawk Democrats I met were equally, if not more, disheartening. Although my meeting with Senator Hillary Clinton (D-NY) went well, I don't believe she will do anything to alleviate the suffering of the Americans in Iraq or the Iraqi people. I don't believe that sending more troops is the solution; it will only aggravate an already unstable situation. We met in New York City with Senator Charles Schumer's aide, who told us that the senator thinks the occupation of Iraq is a "good thing for America," but he wouldn't elaborate on why. The aide was asked if the senator had a vested interest in keeping this war going, because the Senator is certainly not stupid enough to believe that this misbegotten misadventure in the Middle East is good for anyone. I don't think the people of Louisiana, Alabama, and Mississippi, who got little or no relief because of resources diverted to the war, would agree with the senator that this illegal occupation is a "good thing."

The "Antiwar" Democrats perplex me the most, however. Except for the good guys, like the members of the Out of Iraq Caucus and a few senators, the Dem party line is that we must allow Iraq a window of two months' time and, after the referendum on the constitution this month and the parliamentary elections in December, it will be time to attack the failed policies of George and his cabal of liars.

In my meeting with Howard Dean, he told me that the Iraq issue was "hard" and the new Democratic "Contract with America" is going to have ten points, and the first one is going to be "Universal Health Care." I told Dr. Dean that if the Democrats do not come out strongly against the war and against the Bush administration's disastrous policies, they were going to become irrelevant as a party—something that is already happening. I am just hoping against hope that the war is on the Democrats' contract somewhere. Our current president is always saying that sending our children to die and kill is "hard work." I hate to see that same adjective used to describe bringing them home. The war issue is not complicated: wrong to invade and wrong to stay. Bring our troops home. Simple.

If one is not speaking out right now against the killing in Iraq, one is supporting it. I believe that the members of Congress who opposed to this war need our 100 percent support, admiration, and encouragement. Everyone else needs to be prodded in the right direction. I implored every politician I spoke to this past week (and during our bus trip) to lead our country out of the occupation. I believe that if they did, America would follow them through fire to bring our troops home.

Finally, I was harassed at the Capitol Building by a thug security guard who screamed at me to get out of the building until my next appointment. I complained to another security guard about the disrespectful treatment that I had received, and he said that most of the employees were "Republicans" and they didn't appreciate what I was doing. I have news for them: this is not about politics. To me, this is about flesh and blood. This is not about Right and Left, this is about right and wrong. Nineteen soldiers were needlessly killed in Iraq this past week. Nineteen families are now being senselessly and avoidably devastated. Hundreds of innocent Iraqis are being killed just for being home, shopping, or running an errand at the wrong time. We know that, on average, almost three of our young men and women are killed every day, but the number of Iraqis killed each day—civilians like you and me—is not known. While Democrats hem and haw, how many more families will get the news that their children have been senselessly slaughtered?

What are they waiting for?

October 4, 2005

FIVE

I Have Arrived, I Am Home

*"Every day we do things, we are things that have to do with peace.
If we are aware of our life . . . our way of looking at things, we will
know how to make peace right in the moment, we are alive."*
—Thich Nhat Hahn

I WAS RECENTLY HONORED AND HUMBLED TO BE IN
the presence of a holy man, Thich Nhat Hahn, at MacArthur
Park, in a Hispanic neighborhood of Los Angeles.

Thay, or teacher, as he is known, is a Buddhist monk who
worked during the Vietnam War years to bring peace and rec-
onciliation to North and South Vietnam. Martin Luther King,
Jr., nominated him for a Nobel Peace Prize. As he walks he
radiates an aura of peace and acceptance.

In a speech I delivered at Riverside Church in New York City
on the one-year anniversary of Casey's death, which was also
the thirty-seventh anniversary of Martin Luther King, Jr.'s assas-
ination, I said: "We must all do one thing for peace each day.
But that is not enough. We must live peace and embody peace

if we want peace on earth. Our entire lives must be for peace. Not just one activity a day."

Every step is peace.
That was the theme for our walk together in MacArthur Park. Thay reminded us to be in the present, to take every step in peace, and to know that we are walking on the earth in peace. He lovingly admonished the hundreds of people to do everything in peace: eat, walk, talk, breathe, sleep, work, play, etcetera. No yelling, no angry words, no harsh statements. His admonishment struck me to the bone because I have been so strident in my criticism of the Bush administration's abhorrent neglect, public dishonesty, and ruthless violence. There must be a better way now if we truly want our country to be a leader of international peace, justice and dignity, and not an imperial leader of torture, domination, and not war.

I have arrived. I am home.
This was the first sign we passed as we started on our walk. Thay told us to say those phrases with every other step.

I have arrived.
Every second we live is a new arrival in the present. I see so much conflict and struggle in our world because we don't live in this second. We are worried about the next second and mourning the past second. Camp Casey taught me to live each moment in the moment's arrival. One of the reasons I have been able to remain

so calm in the face of an onslaught of troubles is because I realized in Camp Casey that I could not struggle against the current of my life and change my destiny any more than I could bring my son back from the land of the dead. Each second of each day is a precious arrival and we should honor each moment. Another holy man, Jesus Christ, said: "Do not worry about tomorrow; it will have nough worries of its own. There is no need to add to the troubles each day brings."[1]

I am home.

I made a new friend named Jewel, a Buddhist whose son was a medic on the front lines in Iraq and has tried to commit suicide three times since returning from the horror of the war. Jewel is distraught and beside herself with worry. She says her son needs treatment because he is dying, but his superiors will not allow him to be diagnosed for post-traumatic stress disorder (PTSD). As a result, he can't get the help he so desperately needs.

The price that we are paying for this war goes so much deeper than the billions of our tax dollars being squandered by the Pentagon on war, goes so much further than the deterioration of our reputation worldwide. Thousands of families are paying the price with the life, limbs, and sanity of their loved ones. Over 15,000 of our young people are wounded. The Veterans Administration estimates that over 25 percent of our children will come home with post-traumatic stress disorder.[2] I believe that number is higher, because there are many cases, like that of Jewel's son, where the military refuses to allow soldiers to seek treatment for PTSD. Many of them are simply forced back to battle. Even if they are not physically wounded or killed, our soldiers will not come home entirely whole.

I said to Jewel: "You realize your son died in Iraq." She replied: "We have all died because of this war."

She is right. On April 4, 2004, Cindy Sheehan died, but another Cindy Sheehan was born.

The dead Cindy Sheehan lived for her home and family. She kept a neat and tidy house, cooked meals often, did everyone's laundry, entertained friends, laughed more than she cried, worked at various jobs; her family meant the entire world to her. She lived an insulated life filled with Thanksgivings and Christmases and birthdays and other celebrations.

The Cindy Sheehan who was born on 04/04/04 still adores her family above all, but now knows that *the human family* is worth struggling for too. She knows that the lifelong cause of peace with justice is worth leaving her home for. She is ready to struggle, ready to speak out, ready to put her body on the line, ready to *be home* wherever she is.

I pray for Jewel and especially for her son, who realizes that he died in Iraq. He struggles to be a much better "he" than the one who left his loving home and mother and went off to war. Unfortunately, and tragically, Jewel and her son's story is not uncommon.

"In order to rally people, governments need enemies. They want us to be afraid, to hate, so we will rally behind them. And if they do not

have a real enemy, they will invent one in order to mobilize us."
—Thich Nhat Hahn

While looking up sayings by my new friend, I came upon the above. This has been one of my feelings and themes for months. At one point in our country's history we were told that the enemy was "Communism." Now we are told that the enemy is "Terrorism." If terrorism dries up, the military-industrial complex will drum up new enemies—be it bird flu or the rising wave of democratic social movements in Latin America.

President Bush recently stood in front of the nation and said that things were going to be *far worse* in Iraq in the coming months. Why do we let him get away with it? The other night he likened Iraq to World War II. Why do we let him get away with that? Why do we allow our elected officals to sacrifice our young to the war machine? War will stop when we as parents, educators, religious leaders, brothers, sisters, husbands, and wives refuse to allow our loved ones to go to war. I wish I had refused to allow my son to go to Iraq. I wish I had knocked him out and taken him to Canada . . . or anywhere far enough away from the war monster. It is too late for me and my son, but it's not too late for you.

> *"Some people think it's a miracle to walk on water. I think it is a miracle to walk on the earth in peace."*
> —Thich Nhat Hahn

If we don't learn how to do this, we as a people are screwed. We do a good job identifying the problems with the war in Iraq. Now how do we as a people who want to walk on our earth in peace go forward?

Join us in working always for peace, in peace: be peace.
I am dedicating my life and Casey's life to peace. We need to remember that Iraq is not the fifty-first state of the Union. We need to let the Iraqi people live in peace.

How do we do that? Let's walk each step away from the killing, torture, and war, and walk each step in peace towards the answer.

October 10, 2005

SIX

Going to the Movies

GOING TO THE MOVIES WAS SOMETHING CASEY AND I
enjoyed doing together. Casey was a theater arts major in college, and he watched movies with a critical eye. Since I love
sharing my children's passions with them, Casey and I would
see movies together often.

We saw two movies the last time he was home for
Christmas, in 2003, before he was deployed to Iraq. We saw
the third installment in the *Lord of the Rings* trilogy and we saw
Peter Pan—I still have the ticket stub in my wallet. We got to the
theater a little late, so we had to sit up front with the moms
and dads and their small children. I commented to Casey that
it looked like we were the only "grown-ups" interested in the
movie. The small children were cute to watch as they enjoyed

the movie, and Casey and I got quite a few chuckles from them also.

On Ash Wednesday 2004, a few days before Casey left for Iraq, his dad and I went to see *The Passion of the Christ*. That was our Ash Wednesday penance that year. Casey's dad fell asleep during the scourging scene while I sat in my seat and quietly sobbed. I was especially touched by the character that played Jesus' mom who followed her son while he was being violently tortured and killed. Of course, since I became a mom more than twenty-six years ago, I have identified with Mary as she sobbed at the foot of her son's cross and cradled his lifeless body in her arms.

I am recounting all of this because, since Casey was killed in Iraq, I find it extremely difficult to go to the movies. Yesterday, I went to the same movie theater in Vacaville, California, that Casey and I loved to attend. My sister and I saw the movie *Serenity*. It was a good science fiction flick that had many parallels with what is going on in our world today. But that is not what affected me about yesterday's movie going experience.

First of all, it breaks my heart to be in the same theater where Casey and I saw so many films together. While we were waiting for the movie to start, the interminable previews began to roll. About the fourth one in, a preview for the movie *Jarhead* came on. My sister quickly said, "Close your eyes." Well, I already had them closed, and what I heard was tough. I heard a flight attendant tell a planeload of Marines, "Good luck, now" as they got off the plane, I am assuming in Kuwait. I wondered if a smiling flight attendant said the same thing to Casey has he deplaned in

64

Kuwait. I will never know. I can't ask him and he didn't tell me the one phone call I received from him before he was killed five days after he arrived in Baghdad.

Well, that did it for me. I couldn't stop sobbing for twenty minutes after that preview. I tried to do it quietly so as to not disturb the other moviegoers. I wonder how many other theater patrons have been so affected by the preview for *Jarhead*?

God forbid that anyone get too disturbed over the devastation and needless death and suffering in Iraq. God forbid that the media tell us that 32 of our young people have already been slaughtered in Iraq so far this month. God forbid that we have to think about the hundreds of faceless and nameless people who live in Iraq and who have been killed or dismembered too, just going about their everyday lives.

God forbid that anyone be held accountable for the mayhem in the Mideast! God forbid that a broken hearted and honest mother speak from her heart to the lies and betrayals of the Bush administration that makes some war supporters uncomfortable.

As of October 14, 2005, the United States Department of Defense lists 1,963 U.S. soldiers confirmed dead in Iraq and two more pending confirmation for a total of 1,965. Will 2,000 dead U.S. soldiers in Iraq be the wake-up call America needs to order our president to end the war? Whatever number Casey's killing was, his death was a wake-up call for me—a violent and tragic wake-up call. Casey was not a number and neither will the two thousandth or three thousandth soldier be a number to his or her family. Casey was a wonderful young man who loved to go to the movies with his mom. What is the soldier like who is alive right now but is about to be killed? What are the children and moms and dads and old folk and young people in Iraq like who will be slaughtered later today or tomorrow or before the end of the month? Which mom in America or Iraq or Afghanistan will be the next unfortunate one to fall on the floor screaming for her dead loved one?

No, most Americans probably did not sob when they saw the previews for *Jarhead* and most Americans probably didn't go straight to their son's premature grave to place fresh flowers after their movie outing.

I did. God forbid that I am angry and God forbid that I want Bush and Cheney and their supporters held accountable for their war that is robbing us all of so much.

October 14, 2005

SEVEN

Supporting Hillary

I WOULD LOVE TO SUPPORT HILLARY CLINTON'S RUN for president if she would come out against the U.S. occupation of Iraq. But I don't think she will speak out against the occupation because, in fact, she supports it.

I will never make the mistake of supporting another pro-war Democrat for president again, nor will I ever support a pro-war Republican.

The people of this country want the occupation to end. People in Iraq want this occupation to end. The world wants the occupation to end.

Senator Clinton: taking the peace road would not prove that you are weak. Instead, it would prove that you are strong and wise. As a mom, as an American, and as a patriot, I implore you to have the strength and courage to lead the fight for peace.

I want to support you, I want to work with you, but, like many American moms, I will resist your candidacy with every bit of my power and strength unless you show us the wisdom it takes to be a truly great leader.

Prove that you represent the will of the nation and reflect the American people's desire to reject domestic neglect, corporate greed, torture, and war.

Senator Clinton: come out against this occupation of Iraq. Not because it is the politically expedient thing to do, but because it is the *humane* thing to do. If you want to make our dead soldiers' sacrifice count, bring the rest of their buddies home alive.

• • •

ON SEPTEMBER 22, 2005, I MET WITH SENATOR Clinton and Senator Harry Reid. A few days prior to our meeting, I was in Brooklyn and had said Clinton was waiting for a politically "expedient" moment to speak out against the war in Iraq. I of course think the "waiting for the right moment" tactic is wrong, because politics has nothing to do with wanting to end the slaughter going on in Iraq. No one asked the families of Americans, nor those of the tens of thousands of innocent Iraqis who have been killed, what political party they were rooting for. When a mother receives the news that her child has been killed in a war launched by lying politicians, she never thinks, "Oh no, how could this have happened? I am a Democrat/Republican!"

I thought my meeting with Senator Clinton went well. It seemed like she listened and heard what we had to say. I went with another Gold Star Mother, Lynn Braddach, and my sister, Dede Miller. After Senator Reid left, Senator Clinton stayed for a few more moments during which she told us that she had met with other Gold Star Mothers who had different views than ours. I said it didn't really matter, because our view is right. Lynn, Dede, and I don't want our loved ones to be used as political pawns to justify the killing spree in Iraq. I can't believe any mother who has had her heart and soul torn out would not want to try and prevent the same anguish for other mothers.

How often does the dishonesty and corruption of Cheney and Bush's administration have to be exposed before every American—elected official, media representative, average citizen—feels taken for a ride and and says, "Enough is enough, bring our troops home now"?

I thought Mrs. Clinton listened to us, but apparently she didn't, because immediately afterwards she said the following to Sarah Ferguson of the *Village Voice*: "My bottom line is that I don't want their sons to die in vain . . . I don't believe it's smart to set a date for withdrawal . . . I don't think it's the right time to withdraw."[1]

That quote sounds exactly like what the few Republicans I have talked to are saying. Making sure that our children do not die in "vain" sounds exactly like something President Bush says.

A "date" for withdrawal? That sounds like Rush Limbaugh talking; that doesn't sound like an opposition party leader speaking to me. What Senator Clinton is saying sounds exactly like the Republican Party talking points that Senators Dole and McCain dish out.

Senator Clinton was in California recently to raise money for her political campaigns. An invitation to one of her star-studded galas reads: "We must stand with Senator Clinton as she stands up for what we believe in. Hillary is and always has been our champion in the White House and the Senate." It goes on to describe her as one of the "strongest, most passionate and intelligent Democrats."

I didn't get an invitation to any of the events, but maybe that's because she doesn't stand up for what I believe in. Furthermore, I don't believe she is passionate; I think she is a political animal who believes she has to be a Warhawk to keep up with the big boys. She is intelligent—there's no doubt about that. However, I believe that the intelligent thing for Democrats to do in 2006 and 2008 would be to come out strongly and correctly against the botched, bungled, illegal, and immoral occupation of Iraq.

Sixty-two percent of Americans now acknowledge that this war is based on fabrications and betrayals and want our troops home. fifty-three percent of Americans want our troops to come home immediately. The last time I looked, Democrats did not make up sixty-two percent of our population. Americans oppose this war in overwhelming numbers and it crosses party lines. Because America can see that the war in Iraq actually *fuels* terrorism and makes the world and our country *less* secure. Every day more people acknowledge that this is not a "right and left" issue, it is a "right and wrong" issue.

Sixty-nine of our best and brightest have been sent meaninglessly and unnecessarily to their premature deaths since I met with Mrs. Clinton on September 22, 2005. Sixty-nine mothers and fathers and who knows how many spouses, brothers, sisters, sons, daughters, cousins, and friends have been meaninglessly and unnecessarily sent into tailspins of grief and emptiness since that meeting. By the time you read these words, that number will be much higher.

We all know that Senator Clinton, along with many other representatives and senators, voted to give Cheney and Bush the authority to invade a sovereign nation that was no threat to the U.S.A. We know that they spinelessly abrogated their constitutional responsibility and duty in order to declare war. We know—and most of them know—that voting to give an irresponsible person authority to wage war was a devastating mistake. But I know that this knowledge will neither bring back my son or any of the thousands of other people who have been slaughtered. If neither the Democrats nor the Republicans will represent the will of the people, can we even call this place a real democracy?

October 15, 2005

EIGHT

After My Next Arrest

If you believe in what you are doing, give me your stiffest sentence. If you don't, then resign.
—Mahatma Gandhi

YESTERDAY STARTED OFF WITH A BANG WHEN A group of us went to Arlington Cemetery to lay a wreath in the section where the Iraq War dead are buried. In our group were three other members of Gold Star Families for Peace. Juan Torres was with us; his son, also named Juan, was murdered in Afghanistan.

First of all, I was followed all morning by the Park Police— I guess because I am a very dangerous subversive. While I would never hurt a flea, I suppose I *am* dangerous to those who want us to wave the flag and ignore the facts of fabrication and corruption in our government today.

Juan, Beatriz Saldivar, and Julie Cuniglio—who have all had loved ones killed in this war—had brought pictures of their now-dead loved ones with them to Arlington Cemetery. We were told by the administration of the cemetery that they couldn't bring the pictures in because they were "political statements"! We were stunned. Pictures of children who have been ordered into battle by this country and killed on foreign soil can't be shown in a cemetery that supposedly honors them. We are living in a state that orders its children into a war and then calls them political statements. What kind of country are we becoming?

After Arlington, I met with Senator Carl Levin from Michigan, a strong and outspoken critic of the war. The mess that Bush and Cheney have unleashed on our country and on the world weighs heavily on his shoulders. He knows something needs to be done. Let's support him in doing so. I will also meet with Senator Debbie Stabenow from the same state.

We headed to the vigil at the White House and waited long hours in the freezing cold. There was a man there who had several signs, one of which said: "Saddam loves Cindy." This man didn't care that Rumsfeld (or "Rumsfailed" as I accidentally called him in an interview recently) was at one point buddy-buddy with Saddam Hussein and provided him tons of WMDs before he became our enemy. I told this man that he didn't bother me, and he told me I didn't bother him either. Well, if I didn't bother him, why did he come down and make signs and march for hours screaming that I kill our soldiers? We found out why: he was being paid sixty dollars an hour to do so from some non-profit, right-wing group. He said he would switch signs if we gave him more money. What kind of country are we becoming?

At 7:30 p.m., about a hundred Americans symbolically died in front of the White House. When twenty-six of us refused to get up, we were arrested. As usual, the Park Police were very polite and efficient; many of them whispered words of support and encouragement to us. We are planning more die-ins in front of the White House. We call on all Americans to come out and symbolically die with us here in D.C. . . . or do it in your own communities at relevant places: recruitment centers, federal buildings, and outside the offices of elected officials.

When I was being processed out of the jail, the Lieutenant warned me that if I got arrested again I might have to stay in jail for a couple of months, since it was my second arrest and the first one had yet to be be resolved. The lieutenant went to bat for me, he said, so the judge wouldn't hold me this time.

I appreciate the warning of the lieutenant, but I plan on doing civil disobedience again this evening. I cannot live freely in a country where the highest leaders of the land, who are guilty of ordering its young into war on false pretenses, are permitted to continue to lead while others who are exercising their constitutionally protected right to free speech are locked up in jail. I cannot live freely in a country where others are allowed to lie in retaliation against a person who had the temerity to challenge previous lies. I cannot live freely in a country where bereaved family members aren't allowed to carry pictures of their murdered loved ones into a national cemetery.

And in another hand picked audience propaganda speech in front of military spouses, President Bush just said: "This war will require more sacrifice, more time, and more resolve."[1]

And we who believe that this war should end now will continue to make sacrifices, continue to be patient, and will continue in our resolve to counter Bush and Cheney with every fiber of our being. In the end, we will prevail.

Meanwhile, next time I go before a magistrate after my next arrest, I will tell him or her: "If you believe in what you are doing, give me the stiffest sentence possible. If you don't, then resign."

Peace soon.

October 26, 2005

NINE

Open Letter to George Bush's Mama

DEAR BARBARA,

On April 4, 2004, your oldest child, George W. Bush, killed my oldest child, Casey Austin Sheehan.

Unlike your oldest child, my son was a marvelous person who joined the military to serve his country and to try and make the world a better place. Casey didn't want to go to Iraq, but he knew his duty. Your son went AWOL from a glamour unit. George couldn't even handle the Alabama Air National Guard. Casey joined the Army before your son became commander-in-chief. We all know that your son was thinking of invading Iraq as early as 1999. Casey was a dead man before George even became president and before he even joined the Army in May 2000.

I raised Casey and my other children to use their words to solve problems and conflicts. I told my four children from the time that they were small that it is *always* wrong to kick, bite, hit, scratch, or pull hair. If the smaller children couldn't find the words to solve their conflicts without violence, I always encouraged them to find a mediator like a parent, older sibling, or teacher to help them find the words.

Did you teach George to use his words and not his violence to solve problems? It doesn't appear so. Did you teach him that killing other people for profits and oil is *always* wrong? Obviously you did not. I also used to wash my children's mouths out with soap on the rare occasion that they lied. Did you do that to George? Can you do it now? He has lied and he is still lying. Saddam did not have WMDs or ties with Al-Qaeda. The Downing Street memos prove that your son knew this before he invaded Iraq.

On August 3, 2005, your son said that he killed my son and the other brave and honorable Americans for a "noble cause." Well, Barbara, mother to mother, that angered me. I don't consider invading and occupying another country that is not a threat to the U.S.A. to be a noble cause. I don't think invading a country, killing its innocent citizens, and ruining its infrastructure while your family and your family's war-profiteering friends become rich is a noble cause.

So I went down to Crawford in August to ask your son what noble cause he killed my son for. He wouldn't speak with me. I think that showed incredibly bad manners. Do you think a president, even if it is your son, should be so inaccessible to his employers? Especially a boss whose life he has devastated so completely?

I have been to the White House several times since August to try and meet with George and I am going back to Crawford next week. Do you think you can call him and ask him to do the right thing and bring the troops home from the illegal and immoral war he carelessly started? I hear you are one of the few people he still talks to. He won't speak to his father, who knew the difficulties and impossibilities of going into Iraq. If you won't tell him to bring the troops home, can you at least urge him to meet with me?

On March 18, 2003, a little over a year before my dear, sweet Casey was killed by your son's policies, you appeared on *Good Morning America* and said the following: "Why should we hear about body bags and deaths? Oh, I mean, it's not relevant. So why should I waste my beautiful mind on something like that?"[1]

Now I have something to tell you, Barbara. I didn't want to hear about deaths or body bags either. On April 4, 2004, three Army officers came to my house to tell me that Casey had been killed in Iraq. I fell on the floor screaming and begging the cruel Angel of Death to take me too. But the Angel of Death that took my son is your son.

Casey came home in a flag-draped coffin on April 10, 2004. I used to have a beautiful mind too. Now my mind is filled with the image of his beautiful body in his casket and memories of burying my brave and honest boy before his life really began.

Casey's beautiful mind was ended by an insurgent's bullet to his brain, but your son might as well have pulled the trigger.

Besides encouraging your son to have some honesty and courage and to finally do the right thing, don't you think you owe me, and every other Gold Star parent, an apology for the cruel and careless remark you made?

Your son's amazingly ignorant, arrogant, and reckless policies in Iraq are responsible for so much sorrow and trouble in this world.

Can you make him stop? Do it before more mothers' lives are needlessly and cruelly harmed. It has happened too many times already.

Sincerely,

Cindy Sheehan

November 18, 2005

TEN

Blessings

IT WAS HARD TO FEEL BLESSED TODAY AS I SAT at Casey's grave here in Vacaville, California. Sure, a lot of good things have happened in my sphere of influence this year, but the blessings are always tempered by the reason for the blessings.

If Casey had not been killed in the Bush administration's imperialistic war for power and oil, I wouldn't be on this path. I wish to God I weren't on this path. But I am, so here are the blessings I am thankful for this year.

The main blessings that I can thankfully still count are my three surviving children: Carly, Andy, and Janey. They are incredibly wonderful children who didn't ask for the trial that George Bush has given them by murdering their oldest brother.

They didn't ask to have a mom who is away most of the time try-ing to make the world a better place to leave for them. They did-n't ask for it, but they are handling everything with the courage and integrity that are the hallmarks of Sheehan children.

I can look at the events of the past week or so and be thank-ful that some Democrats are finally displaying a modicum of courage in speaking out against the war and in favor of bring-ing the troops home from this monstrosity. I hope that the Democrats will finally unite against the immoral occupation of Iraq, which has put an empty place at the holiday tables of over 2,100 American families.

I can also hope against hope that the war criminals in power, who advocate and condone torture, and who use the same chemical weapons against innocent Iraqis that they accused Saddam of using, will finally have to resign in dis-grace before a mostly complicit Congress has to impeach them. After Cheney, George and Co. resign in shame, someone needs to haul them off to The Hague for war crime trials. That would be something to celebrate.

I am especially thankful for the inspiration that led me to Crawford in August to confront the criminal on his own turf. I am thankful to George, who very predictably did not meet with me and so sparked the Camp Casey peace movement. I am extremely appreciative of the thousands of Americans who came out to Camp Casey during our miraculous three-week stay. I am gratified by the millions of citizens who stood behind us with their prayers and support. The peace movement is gaining momentum and we will see our troops come home soon. This fact is overwhelmingly miraculous to me.

I have met so many amazing, loving, and delightful people since I started my quest to end the occupation of Iraq. My Gold Star Families are especially dear to me. They have found a way to bring their horrible grief to the forefront of the American consciousness, and to help America see the terrible price that some of us have had to pay. One of my Gold Star Moms had her son commit suicide two years ago as George was smirkingly serving plastic turkey. Another dad got in touch with me this week to tell me that they are burying their son on the Saturday after Thanksgiving this year. The Gold Star Families for Peace are handling their losses with grace, courage, and integrity. The Bush crime family and their cronies can take lessons from them. This administration has ruined the holidays for so many people worldwide, I don't know how they can choke down their turkey.

I am profoundly grateful for the life of my son Casey Austin. He lived his life with grace, courage, and integrity. His life is a model for me in my resolve to bring his buddies home alive. Unlike George, Casey never got anything handed to him on a silver platter. Casey put himself on a silver platter and handed his young life over to save the lives of his buddies. I am not grateful for the way he died, or that so many others will also come home in flag-draped coffins, too. The atrocity has to end before another family experiences the emptiness of a chair at another family table.

Since Camp Casey, I do have hope that one of these days our holidays will have real joy and laughter again. I have hope that America is ready to take back our rights, freedoms, and responsibilities. I have hope that people will be held accountable for the needless death and destruction they have caused the world. I am intensely grateful for the return of hope.

I also have high hopes that we are at a unique point in history where we will be able to change the paradigm of our existence from one of perpetual war and killing to one of perpetual love and peace. This will be the best blessing that a mom could ever ask for. Maybe next year.

November 24, 2005

ELEVEN

Open Letter to President George W. Bush

GEORGE,

My family is spending our second Thanksgiving without Casey thanks to you and your lies. I am spending the day crying on a plane on my way to Crawford, coming again to ask you for a meeting.

I was in Crawford for three weeks in the summer and in D.C. several times asking for a meeting with you, and now I am returning to our vacation home to try once again. I don't know why you like Crawford so much, but I love it because of the Camp Casey Peace Community that arose during August this year. When I arrived back here at the Peace House I felt a sense of coming home, belonging to something that is far greater than any of us: a community that is filled with love, acceptance, and peace. Is this what you feel when you return frequently to Crawford? Also, the beautiful Texas sunset stirred memories of our days at Camp Casey when we would close our activities each day with ex-Marine Jeff Key playing taps among the crosses that honored our fallen. August was a miraculous time.

In August, I wanted to ask you this question: For what noble cause did you kill Casey and the others? Since then hundreds more of our brave young men and women have been killed in the charade of Iraq. We can only guess how many innocent Iraqis have been slaughtered. You still have not answered my question. Many people in our country who have had sons or daughters killed, people who have sons and daughters serving, and many concerned Americans want to know that answer to that question too.

Also, since August we have discovered that American forces are using chemical weapons in Iraq. The Army admitted that white phosphorous was used as an offensive weapon against "enemy combatants." Oh, really, George, since when did a weapon fired from a distance distinguish between enemies and innocents? Especially when it is so hard for soldiers on the ground to differentiate between enemies and innocents? It is hard for one to ignore the grisly pictures of the burned citizens of Fallujah.

By the way, George, isn't the use of chemical weapons prohibited? Don't you always say that "Saddam is a bad man" for using chemical weapons on his own people? Does that mean, then, that it is okay for you to use chemical weapons because the citizens of Iraq are not "your people"? Saddam should be on trial for killing so many innocent people. Bombing cities where innocent civilians live and using chemical weapons are war crimes. Doesn't that make you a war criminal? Move over, Saddam. There is a new bad guy in town.

George, for the sake of the Iraqi people, don't you think it is time to bring our military forces home? It is time to stop using killing to force your idea of freedom and democracy. Do you know the kind of freedom and democracy you like? Where no open dissent is allowed, no one is able to petition the government for redress of wrongs, where our e-mails can be read and our library reading materials checked up on and analyzed? Your kind of freedom and democracy smears brave patriots as cowards and traitors for daring to speak out against your murderous policies. A majority of Americans doesn't even want your brand of so-called freedom and democracy. What makes you think the Iraqi people want it?

George, for the sake of our wonderful, brave, and very young people who proudly wear the uniform of the U.S.A., it is time to bring them home. They have done everything you have asked of them. They have also done things that have made at least one quarter of them very sick in their hearts and souls. Some of them have been so needlessly and avoidably killed and some of them are coming home with pieces missing. For what, George? What noble cause?

George, I don't blame you for using your family influence to get out of serving in Vietnam. I don't blame anyone for trying to get out of that disastrous and totally evil war. What I do blame you for is killing my son in another disastrous and evil war. Casey was willing to serve his country and to die to save his buddys' lives. You should be ashamed of yourself for exploiting Casey's honor and the honor of everyone in our armed forces. Ask your vice president if he thinks that Casey may have had other "priorities" besides dying at twenty-four. Ask your mama if her "beautiful mind" is bothered yet. Mine is.

Did you have the sacred luxury of having your two daughters at home with you today for Thanksgiving dinner? Did you lovingly tease them during the meal like my family used to do? Did you tell old funny family stories and laugh about old times? Did you, George? Our family did share a meal together and we tried to be merry, but you know what? It's not the same. Casey's death put a damper on all of our days, but the holidays are especially hard.

Are you and Laura going to hit the sack tonight and toss and turn or stare out of the window worried that Jenna or Barbara may be killed? Are you going to jump at every single telephone ring, or run to the door with your hearts beating wildly at every knock, fearing the Angel of Death in an Army uniform? I didn't think so. Two soldiers were killed today in Iraq, George. I hope to God their families aren't just sitting down to enjoy their meal when the grim reapers come to tell them their holidays are ruined forever. There is no good time for such horrendous news.

I ask you to again do the right thing.

Bring our troops home from Iraq. How many deaths do you think will be necessary before Casey's is "justified"? 58,000? One was too many.

I will tell you what noble cause Casey died for, George: true and lasting peace. Please dignify all of the deaths by finally stopping the barbaric killing before you ruin too many more holidays for way too many more people.

Sincerely,

Cindy Sheehan

November 24, 2005

TWELVE

Mi Familia de Corazón

Camp Casey Thanksgiving, Crawford, Texas

I WAS FEELING VERY DOWN WHEN I WAS FLYING
to Waco from Sacramento yesterday. I did a lot of crying and
missing Casey on the way. I am not yet at the place in my grieving where I can look at all of our good times and feel grateful
for them. Remembering many, many happy Thanksgivings
only made me feel worse.

So, when I was on a short layover in Dallas I called my
sister—one of the Crawford Twelve jailbirds—to ask her who
was picking me up. She wouldn't give me a straight answer.
She would only say, "Don't worry, someone will be there." I
told her not to worry about it, I would take a taxi to the Peace
House or rent a car. I was *definitely* feeling sorry for my poor
little self.

Well, after the very short flight from Dallas, and after a luggage misunderstanding on the tarmac, I walked into the terminal in Waco. Lo and behold, there were dozens of people there to welcome me, and lots of press. Most of the people, including the press, were old Camp Casey friends. My spirits were lifted and I felt strangely at home.

After a stop at the Peace House we headed back out to Camp Casey on the Camp Casey II location. We stayed up for hours talking about politics, the war, old times, and the future. We laughed and cried and I thought: I am so lucky to have two families. My children and *mi familia de corazón*—my family of the heart.

Both of my families are very close and loving—we laugh and have good times—but our good times are hampered by the fact that we are here for starkly serious reasons. We want to hold the President and his administration accountable for *willfully* misleading the country in to war, and we want to end the disasterous occupation. Some of us are also here because we have been so intimately and tragically affected by the government's mistakes. We periodically stop to reflect on these things.

When I am here in Crawford at Camp Casey, I almost feel sorry for President Bush in his protected Green Zone. He is protected from physical harm (which he need not fear from us) and he is protected from political harm. He doesn't have to face the people who vehemently disagree with his policies and who oppose his continued killing. He is protected from the real world of pain and need. He has never had to face his failures or own up to anything.

The reason I feel sorry for him though, is that he has few friends or confidants. Reports show that he only has four people who he can talk to. He is not even on friendly terms with his father, Karl Rove, or Vice President Dick Cheney. We at Camp Casey, on the other hand, are surrounded by laughter, love, hope and acceptance. One can't help smiling just being here.

I received an e-mail today with the subject line: "Throw the Bitch in the Ditch." The writer accused me of "throwing dirt" on Casey, himself, and his son, all of whom have served the country. I have *never* said anything to disparage the honorable service of Casey or the others who have enlisted in the military. The email's writer didn't even blink an eye at calling the mother of a war hero a "bitch." I wonder how he feels about his own leadership "throwing dirt" on the service of actual military men like John Kerry, Jack Murtha, Max Cleland, and, yes, even John McCain. I have never questioned people who try to stay alive fighting in the dishonorable wars started by old men. The ones I appreciate even more, though, are the people of courage who resist killing innocent people and become conscientious objectors.[1] I wish my son had. I like to believe that would have happened. He told everyone before he left for Iraq that he didn't think he could kill anyone.

Someone has to make George face his failures and change his ways. We in the Camp Casey Peace movement are dedicated to that mission. But more importantly we are dedicated to the mission of honoring our fallen heroes by bringing their buddies home alive.

We will keep pressing; we will not give up; we will stay the course; we will prevail.

November 25, 2005

THIRTEEN

Comfort Zones

TODAY WAS BITTERLY COLD AS I WALKED FROM THE Charing Cross Tube Station to Parliament Square in London. I was heading there with my traveling companion, Julie, to visit Brian Haw after several productive days in England and Scotland.

Brian is a peace activist and exceptionally compassionate man who has been camping out and holding a vigil in Parliament Square since June 2, 2001. He was so enraged by the United Nations sanctions against Iraq he felt compelled to camp in Parliament Square as an act of public protest.

While I was holding my vigil and camping outside George Bush's vacation home in Crawford, Texas, Brian sent me a letter. Part of it reads:

We stand beside you as family, and you can be sure of our love no matter what. Now let's help the rest to understand, sort the mess in the quickest possible time. I don't want another day to go by, another child to come home in a body bag, nor do you. Well, let's get through to the rest of our folks pretty damn quick. Amen?!

Your brother Brian, in Jesus's name

The letter so touched me that I knew if I ever visited England, I would have to go and see Brian. I was shocked when I found out that Brian, after peacefully camping there for four years, was arrested early Saturday morning.

This past year, the British Parliament passed a very restrictive law called the Serious Organised Crime and Police Act 2005. The act restricts freedom of speech and freedom of assembly around Parliament and No. 10 Downing Street. Citizens who break this law can be arrested and often are.

A young woman went in front of the Parliament building and read the names of the ninety-seven British soldiers who had been killed in Iraq as of that day. She too was arrested.

An old man started yelling at British Foreign Secretary Jack Straw for his complicity in war crimes. The man was arrested.

Brian is allowed to be there because the law was passed after his vigil started, but he was arrested for encouraging "new people" to join his vigil. These new people, naturally, agree that the war is a tragic mistake and that our troops need to come home.

These prohibitions of free speech and dissent are eerily familiar to me. To date, I have been hauled in twice for exercising my First Amendment freedoms in America. I have tried to petition my government on dozens of occasions to redress the wrongs that Cheney, Bush, and the other neocons have inflicted on the world and my family. I have spent a lot of money, sacrificed so much, and have traveled far and wide to do so. Few in the government are listening.

When I spoke to a large crowd of hundreds of peace activists in London at an International Peace Conference, I challenged them to take back the freedoms that our governments are taking away from us. Thousands of people traveled from all over the world to join us at Camp Casey over the summer. I wondered why more people in the U.K. haven't gone to Parliament to scream out the names of slaughtered British war heroes after a young woman was arrested for doing the same. Parliament's complicity contributed to the killing of troops and innocent Iraqis. The members of Parliament and Tony Blair should be faced with their acts of murder on a daily basis.

Why, when Brian was arrested the other day, didn't hundreds of people go down to Parliament Square and pitch their tents alongside his?

Why do we as Americans turn the channel when we see that our government is transporting alleged criminals to torture them on European soil?

Why do we turn our backs on the innocent children who are killed everyday in the name of "freedom and democracy"?

Why do we let the war criminals rape and pillage our treasury and steal precious human treasure from our communities and families?

Brian Haw, who is a father of seven, left the comfort zone of his home and family to save the children of the world. He states his reasons so eloquently on his website: "I want to go back to my own kids and look them in the face again knowing that I've done all I can to try and save the children of Iraq and other countries who are dying because of my government's unjust, amoral, fear- and money-driven policies. These children and people of other countries are every bit as valuable and worthy of love as my precious wife and children."[1] I was violently ripped out of my comfort zone on April 4, 2004. Even if I wasn't constantly traveling and demonstrating against the immoral occupation of Iraq, I will never be comfortable again. I will live the rest of my life with a part of my heart and soul missing. I have had my comfort cruelly amputated as so many soldiers have had limbs ripped off by increasingly powerful "improvised explosive devices"— roadside bombs.

Brian showed me pictures of babies who are affected by depleted uranium sickness in Iraq. He showed me pictures of morbidly ill Iraqi children who couldn't or can't get medicine because of either the prior inhumane sanctions or the current occupation. Even as the occupation authorities live in relative security in Baghdad's Green Zone, the people of Iraq have no comfort zones. Their plight goes unrecorded and unreported.

In the eyes of their occupiers, they simply don't count. Their accidental deaths literally go uncounted.

So we who care about freedom and democracy, we who care about our governments' crimes against humanity, must take action. We have to do as Henry David Thoreau said and "vote with our whole ticket."

If you are doing nothing for peace and justice in the world, then start doing something. If you are doing something, then do more. Our survival on this planet demands immediate action.

Now is the time to leave our comfort zones and make a difference.

If you don't know what to do, contact me at campcaseymom@yahoo.com and I'll give you some ideas.

December 11, 2005

FOURTEEN

Language of the Heart

WHILE I WAS IN EUROPE RECENTLY I WAS TOASTED by the mayor of London, Ken Livingston, and greeted by foreign ministers, a vice president, and members of the various Parliaments.

My highest honor now, however, is meeting with the families of children murdered in the U.S. War of Terror.

It doesn't matter if we speak Spanish or American-accented English or a heavy Glasgow accent, like my sister in sorrow, Rose Gentle. Her son Gordon was killed by Blair and Bush in Iraq in July 2004. Our hearts all speak the same idiom of pain. We sing the same lament of futile loss.

In Scotland, as we were meeting with Ministers of Parliament and urging them to withdraw Scottish troops from Iraq, I met a woman named Sue Smith. Her son Philip was killed in Iraq this past July. Her voice resonated with incalculable loss as she spoke of the betrayal that she felt at burying her son too early and for the lies of her prime minister. The wound in her heart was fresh and openly bleeding. In her wounded eyes I saw my heart as it was about a year ago.

At the International Peace Conference in London, I met Shaun Brierly's dad, Peter. Shaun was in the British Army and was killed in the very early days of the war—March 2003. Peter lugged my heavy satchel around London with quiet good humor. In his heavy Yorkshire accent he tried to describe to me what losing his son has done to him and his family. We drank a pint to our boys and to our hurt, but especially to our hearts' resolve to end this war. Through our blinked-back tears we promised each other we would stay strong.

Also at the Peace Conference were Reg Keys and John Miller. Reg's son Tom was killed in action, along with John's son Simon. We attended a few events together and I teased them about the suits they were wearing. They teased me about my "gym clothes." Reg ran against Tony Blair for Prime Minister last year and made a respectable showing. John and Reg are hanging in together with their pain. It is so hard for dads. It is sometimes easier for us moms to express our heart pain than it is for the dads, who often try to head off their heartache at the pass. I also met Ann Laurence, who described her beautiful English countryside home to me and showed me pictures of her handsome son, Marc. She had a quiet voice and eyes filled with heaviness and tears ready to overflow at any moment.

In Spain, I met two more women whose sons were murdered by the policies of our two governments.

Maribel Permuy is the mother of slain Spanish cameraman José Couso. José was murdered in the Palestine Hotel on April 8, 2003, along with another journalist, Taras Protsiuk. I find it so hard to believe that Jose's murder was an accident. In fact, a Spanish magistrate has indicted the three U.S. soldiers who fired a missile at the hotel. The one who should be indicted, though, is President Bush.

Maribel speaks not one word of English and I speak very little Spanish, but our hearts are connected in sorrow and hope. I have been called "*Madre Coraje*"—Mother Courage—in Spain and Latin American countries. However, Maribel is *Madre Mas Coraje*. She has steely and uncompromising resolve to see justice done for her son José. Her love for him and her other children gives her the strength to fight against her government and mine. We laughed and cried so much together, I wonder how we could have communicated any better even if we spoke the same language.

I also met Pilar Mahon in Madrid. Her son, Daniel, was killed in the terrorist bombings of March 11, 2004. The day I met her would have been Daniel's twenty-second birthday. Her nose and eyes were red from a day of mourning her son. She could barely speak, but when she did, her voice rose in anger against President Bush and Spain's former President

José María Aznar, who took our countries to war. The same falsehoods of "fighting them over there, so we don't have to fight them over here" killed both Casey and Daniel. When I meet a woman like Pilar—who spent days weeping at her child's resting place instead of celebrating his birthday—I am filled with outrage. In spite of her constant longing for Daniel, Pilar is leading the fight in Spain for the rights of the families affected by the March 11 terrorist attack.

There are so many people in this world who will be experiencing sorrow-filled holidays this year and every year from now on. It is so painful to remember the Christmas mornings when the kids would rise before the sun came up and beg Mom and Dad to get up too so they could open what Santa had brought them. It is too painful to get out the decorations and hang the one sock that will remain empty for eternity. So most of us skip the traditional Christmas and do whatever we can to support each other through the devastation that our lives have become. Devastation that is so needless and avoidable.

President Bush and the other purveyors of pain can take a day off from spying on Americans without due process to celebrate the holidays with their families. Vice President Cheney made a "surprise" visit to Iraq the other day. Does his heart feel pain for the tragic loss of life that he is causing? How much profit will his company Halliburton and the other war companies earn from all this?

The pain that the Cheney/Bush administration is causing the world is inestimable. The people of the world want an accounting of the pain, they want the officials who seem to be getting off scot-free to be brought to justice for the damage they have wrought on humanity.

However you celebrate your holidays—helping the needy, praying, lighting candles, fasting, giving gifts, cooking meals for family—please remember the families who will be trying to enjoy the holiday season with a part of them missing. But most of all, please remember the people—Iraqi, Afghani, European, American, and others—in harm's way for the old lies and the new lies that seem to surface weekly with each new government scandal.

In conclusion, this is an excerpt from an e-mail I received from a mother in Iraq whose son, Zaydoun Mamoun Fadhil Al-Samarai, a Shi'a insurgent, was involved in the same battle in which Casey was killed. Zaydoun was later killed.

We, my friend, in the march of pain could work together, each from where she is toward putting an end to the bloodshed and toward peace and love to prevail, instead of war.

We could, my lady, work together toward peace and toward putting an end to the bloodshed and give all mothers a hope for happiness because we experience pain when we lost our sons. Because he who did not experience pain cannot understand happiness.

I will be very happy when the war ends so we can celebrate in my town, Samara, which witnessed the birth of my oldest son, Zaydoun, whom I thought would mourn me when I die, but, unfortunately, I mourned him one month before his wedding.

I am conveying his fiancée's greeting, who is still mourning him.

At the end, please accept my deepest sympathies, from a mother who lost her son to another mother who lost her son.

I hope to be able to meet with you on the march for peace and love.

George Bush and the others have taught too many people in this world the language of pain by their lies and their doctrines of preemptive killing for profit.

We need to learn a new language of peace and love that we can speak, even shout, at our leaders who only understand the language of greed and murder.

Peace, shalom, paz, salaam.

December 22, 2005

FIFTEEN

The Opposite of Good Is Apathy

The apathy of the people is enough to make every statue leap from its pedestal and hasten the resurrection of the dead.
—William Lloyd Garrison

THE APATHY OF MOST OF AMERICA IS STUNNING to me. When I found this quote I was filled with wide-eyed wonder that there is one pedestal left in America complete with its original statue, or one grave or tomb still occupied.

On October 26, as MoveOn.org was holding candlelight vigils across the country to mourn the death of the two thousandth American soldier in Iraq, I and two dozen others were being arrested in front of the White House while protesting the carnage done in our name.

Counting the eleventh American soldiers who were most recently killed, the American "official" death toll today is up to 2,193: 200 more families wrecked in less than three months.

My son Casey was among the first 1,000 to be killed in Iraq. We reached that dismal mark by September 2004. MoveOn.org conducted candlelight vigils for that occasion. Then a little over a year later, MoveOn.org conducted candlelight vigils to commemorate the 2,000th soldier. If we don't get off our collective apathetic and complacent backsides to stop the barbaric killing in Iraq, when will the next candlelight vigil be? Bush and Cheney are killing our precious soldiers at the rate of 2.78 per day. By my calculations, we will be lighting our candles again and singing "Kumbaya" by October 2006.

This essay is not an indictment of MoveOn.org, which does some amazing work and was a big supporter of Camp Casey. But my point is this, America: the longer we let the administration of Cheney and Bush to continue, the more our collective humanity is damaged. Apparently, candlelight vigils do very little to stop, or even slow down a little, the carnage committed by the war criminals in D.C.

Then we have the unfortunate civilians of Iraq. I have heard reports that as many as 200 were killed yesterday alone. If 200 were reported, one has to really wonder what the true count was. Bill O'Reilly and President Bush define a terrorist as someone who "kills innocent men, women, and children." Am I the only one who sees the irony and stunning hypocrisy in this statement? Who do the leaders of the free world think are being killed in Iraq? A well-trained and organized army? Terrorists? This is who is being killed in Iraq: living breathing human beings—identical to Americans, or any other human beings anywhere on earth—who are just trying to go about their lives, trying to survive in a war-torn country that was never a threat to America or to "our way of life."

"I would say 30,000 more or less have died as a result of the initial incursion and the ongoing violence against Iraqis," said George on December 12, 2005.[1] Even if one accepts the president's very low guesstimate, his policies have been responsible for ten times the 3,000 deaths on September 11, 2001. By his own admission, he is ten times the killer that Mohammad Atta was. If the White House says 30,000, who knows what the true total is. It fills me with sorrow and hurts my heart to even contemplate such a number.

America, this is what we are allowing our government to do in our name:

- Indefinitely detain and torture prisoners without due process.
- Use chemical weapons and highly toxic depleted uranium on other members of humanity.
- Spy on Americans without a court order.
- Bomb cities filled with human beings like ourselves.
- Attack the infrastructure of other countries.
- Neglect America's most needy (as we saw in New Orleans).
- Steal our tax revenue from the Treasury for use in war.
- Degrade the environment. Et cetera, et cetera, ad nauseum.

Hillary Clinton told me that the "wheels of government grind slowly." This is unacceptable blather. It is time for us wide-awake Americans to end the war.

As long as our elected officials let this senseless war grind on, we will keep the pressure on. We'll continue to organize, continue to agitate, and continue this country's long and inspired tradition of change from below. Protests and civil disobedience will continue at recruiting stations, at federal buildings, at military bases, and at the officies of elected officials.

We will not stop until the war does.

January 6, 2006

SIXTEEN

Matriotism

It is not for him to pride himself who loveth his own country, but rather for him who loveth the whole world. The earth is but one country and mankind its citizens.

—Baha'u'llah

AS MUCH AS I WISH I COULD TAKE CREDIT FOR THE WORD "Matriotism," I got the concept from another woman who recently wrote to me. I was so intrigued by the word that I have been meditating on the possible ideology behind it, and how it might catalyze a new paradigm for true and lasting peace in the world.

Before we dive into the concept of Matriotism, let's first explore the word "patriotism." Dictionary.com defines it as "love of country and willingness to sacrifice for it." When will we all know that patriotism in the U.S. has come to mean exploiting others' love for country by sending them off to kill and be killed to protect the interests of the rich?

There have been volumes written about patriotism, defining it and supporting it, challenging the notion of it. I believe the notion of patriotism has been expediently and nefariously exploited, and has been used to lead our nation into scores of disastrous wars. The idea of patriotism has virtually wiped out entire generations of our precious young people and has allowed our nation's leaders to commit mass murder on an unprecedented scale. The vile sputum of "If you aren't with us, then you are against us" is basically the epitome of so-called patriotism run amok. After the tragedy of 9/11 we we had an opportunity to become a fledgling Matriotic society. Instead, the Bush administration exploited patriotism to fulfill their goals of world domination.

This sort of patriotism begins when we enter kindergarten and learn the Pledge of Allegiance. It transcends all sense when we are taught "The Star Spangled Banner," a hymn to war. In our history classes, the genocide of the Native American peoples is glossed over. Instead we learn about the spread of American imperialism over our continent. In the 1840s, the doctrine of Manifest Destiny was expanded to justify the U.S. conquest and "civilizing" of Mexican territories and Native American populations. Manifest Destiny sought to spread "the boundaries of freedom" to the American Continent— a fever driven by the notion that we have a special mission from God. Sound familiar?

All through school we are brainwashed into believing that our leaders are somehow always right, and that they have our best interests at heart. As Samuel Johnson said, patriotism is the "last refuge of a scoundrel."

Matriotism is the opposite of patriotism. A yin to its yang, a counterforce to the violent militarism of patriotism.

Not everyone is a mother, but there is one universal truth that no one can dispute no matter how hard they try: everyone has a mother. Mothers give life, and, if a child is lucky, mothers nurture life. If a man has a nurturing mother, he will have a base of Matriotism.

A Matriot loves his or her country. A Matriot knows that this country can do a lot of things right, especially when the government is not involved. I know of no other citizens of any country who are more personally generous than those of America. However, a Matriot also knows that when her country is wrong, it can be responsible for murdering thousands upon thousands of innocent and unsuspecting humans. A true Matriot would never bomb cities and villages, or control drones from thousands of miles away to kill innocent men, women and children.

In addition to the above, the most important thing that a Matriot would never do, and this is the key: a Matriot would never send her child or another mother's child to fight nonsense wars. She would march into war herself to protect her child from harm. Matriots fight their own battles but take a dim view of having to do so, and seldom resort to violence to solve conflict. Patriots cower behind the flag and send young people to die for the sake of material wealth.

Women flocked to Camp Casey in August 2005 to work for peace, and have been instrumental in building the Camp Casey movement that has emerged since. Men who are in touch with the Matriot inside of them have been equally instrumental in working to end war.

Everyday Matriots are coming up with new ways to educate and advance peace. Here's a recent example: CODE PINK, endorsed by Gold Star Families for Peace, is calling for an International Day of Peace on March 8—organized by and supported by women. Women and men with matriotic tendencies can get more info and endorse the call for peace at www.womensaynotowar.org. It is time for Matriots to get together and stridently call for an end to the bloodshed.

Meanwhile, I know one thing from the bottom of my heart: My son, Casey, who was an Eagle Scout and a true American patriot, was not served well by his idea of patriotism. I will never forgive myself for not counteracting the false patriotism he was raised on.

I also know that the women of the world who don't have a voice are counting on us women who do have voices to use them. We can end the Bush administration's doctrine of preemptive aggression.

War will end forever when we stand up and say: "We will never give another child to the war machine."

Matriotism above all is a commitment to truth and a commitment to celebrate the dignity of all life.

January 22, 2006

SEVENTEEN

Another World Is Possible

A NEW WORLD IS POSSIBLE . . . AND NECESSARY! This was the theme of the 2006 World Social Forum that I—and tens of thousands of people from around the world—recently attended in Caracas, Venezuela. The idea of a world where everyone lives in peace and with justice is very "subversive," but it is close to the heart and soul of millions around the world.

We need a new world. This one is broken.

Before Casey was killed I never traveled much to speak of. I had gone to Israel and Mexico, and that was about it. I had a barely used passport.

Since I began speaking out against the U.S. occupation of Iraq, I have journeyed all over the United States and now am starting to fill my passport with stamps.

Our world is so beautiful and the people who inhabit it are, for the most part, loving. All they want is a good life for themselves and their children. They want to feel safe and secure in their communities. They want to be warm and not go hungry. They want clean drinking water. They want to dance and laugh. They want to live long lives with their families, and they want their children to bury them at the end of their time here. In short, the people of the world want the same things that we Americans want.

It is governments who demonize and marginalize other cultures, religions, races, and ethnic groups. President Bush and his cohorts want to "fight them over there so we don't have to fight them over here!" Who is this "them" that we are fighting over there? Is it a baby lying in her crib when a bomb is dropped on her house? Is it the mother who has gone shopping for her family's daily food and is killed by a car bomber? Is it a car bomber who never even thought to commit such a heinous act until his country was occupied by a foreign invader? Is it the grandmas and grandpas who are too old, or too stubborn, to leave their lifelong homes while the coalition troops are carpet-bombing their region?

We as citizens of the United States of America must stop allowing our leaders to give orders to kill innocent people. I almost said: we must stop allowing our leaders to "kill" innocent people. But we all know that people like Vice President Cheney don't fight their own fantasy battles or risk losing their own children by shipping them off to Afghanistan or Iraq. No, they order our children to go over and do their dirty work.

Our soldiers are taught that "Hajis," the brown-skinned people of Iraq who clean their toilets and showers and wash their clothes, are less than people. This enables U.S. soldiers to kill them more easily. The dehumanization of non-Americans is also dehumanizing our soldiers. Our children.

I once received hate mail from a "patriotic American" who wrote that, when we see Iraqi mothers and fathers of Iraq screaming because their babies have been killed, they "are just acting for the cameras. They are animals who don't care about their children because they know they can produce another." This mentality is not far off from that of General Sherman, who said "the only good Indian is a dead Indian." Such racist rhetoric dehumanizes us all.

A new world is necessary and it can only be possible if we live the belief that every human being is inherently equal to ourselves. They feel pain when they are hurt. They have hunger pains when they haven't eaten. Their mouths go dry when they are thirsty. They mourn when they experience a loss. They shiver when they are cold. They laugh when they are happy. How can we permit our leaders to get away with killing so many of our brothers and sisters around the world? Iraq Body Count estimates that, as of February 2006, between 28,000 and 32,000 civilians—people like you and me—have been killed in Iraq since the U.S. invasion and occupation began.

A new world is necessary and it can only be possible if we rein in the depraved corporations that earn a profit from the killing.

War profiteers like Halliburton, Bechtel, and General Electric are racking up obscene profits for themselves and their shareholders as they plunder the planet. Conscienceless companies such as Dow are dumping chemicals and other pollutants into the water and atmosphere that sicken people, our environment, and our future! Companies like Wal-Mart are exploiting workers around the world to enrich one family instead of funding health care or a living wage for all of its employees.

A new world is necessary and it can only be possible if we decrease our dependency on oil and use some of the money that we are pouring into the desert sands and sewers of Iraq to expand research on renewable energy sources and expand the renewable sources we already have, such as biodiesel.

A new world is necessary but not possible until the United States gets over the arrogant idea that it can fix the disaster it's created in Iraq and elsewhere alone. We have to reach out to people around the world to forge the bonds that are crucial to protecting innocent members of humankind who are impoverished or killed by our government and the corporations that are largely unchecked.

Peace and justice are intimately connected and the world can't have one without the other. True and lasting peace can only occur when we the people force out leadership that is dependent on the war machine for their jobs and demand justice for the crimes against humanity they perpetrate on on a daily basis.

A new world is possible and it is attainable. For this new world to become a reality it is necessary for us to take into our beings what Martin Luther King, Jr. said of his own eulogy, and more importantly, the way he lived his life:

> I'd like somebody to mention that day, that Martin Luther King, Jr., tried to give his life serving others. I'd like for somebody to say that day, that Martin Luther King, Jr., tried to love somebody. I want you to say that day, that I tried to be right on the war question. I want you to be able to say that day, that I did try, in my life, to clothe those who were naked. I want you to say, on that day, that I did try, in my life, to visit those who were in prison. I want you to say that I tried to love and serve humanity. Yes, if you want to say that I was a drum major, say that I was a drum major for justice; say that I was a drum major for peace; I was a drum major for righteousness.[1]

January 26, 2006

Notes

COVER PHOTOGRAPH

The following notes on David Turnley's cover photograph are quoted from
Media Ethics Issues and Cases, 2nd ed., ed. Philip Patterson and Lee Wilkins
(Madison, WI: WCB Brown & Benchmark, 1994) pp. 212–15, reproduced at
Military Censorship of Photographs by Paul Lester. The BBC website also has
a great direct quote from Turnley here:
http://news.bbc.co.uk/1/hi/world/americas/4290906.stm

One highly emotional picture that did get through military censors
was taken by *Detroit Free Press* photographer David Turnley. Turnley
was riding with the 5th MASH medical unit inside Iraq. A fierce
firefight had recently erupted between Saddam Hussein's
Republican Guard and the 24th Mechanized Infantry Division.
Turnley's helicopter filled with medical personnel and equipment
touched down about 100 yards from a frantic scene. An American
military vehicle had just taken a direct hit. Soldiers on the ground
were upset as they said it had mistakenly been struck by a U.S.
tank. The wounded were quickly retrieved from the vehicle and
carried to the helicopter. Sgt. Ken Kozakiewicz, suffering from a
fractured hand, slumped into the helicopter. The body of the
driver of Kozakiewicz's vehicle was placed on the floor of the helicopter inside a zippered bag. A medical staff member, perhaps
thoughtlessly, handed the dead driver's identification card to
Kozakiewicz. Turnley, sitting across from the injured soldier,
recorded the emotional moment with his camera when
Kozakiewicz realized that his friend was killed by the blast. Later
at the hospital, Turnley asked the soldiers their names. He also
asked if they would mind if the pictures were published. They all

told him to get the images published. The rules of combat
enforced by the military required that Turnley give his film to military officials for approval for publication. A day after the incident,
Turnley learned that his editors had not yet received his negatives
from the Defense Department officials. Military officials insisted
that they were holding onto the film because the images were of a
sensitive nature. They also said that they were concerned about
whether the dead soldier's family had been informed of his death.
Because of Turnley's argument that the family must have been
informed by then, the officials released his film. His photographs
were eventually published in Detroit and throughout the world.
The picture of Kozakiewicz crying over the loss of his friend was
called the "Picture of the War" on the cover of *Parade* magazine.
Several months after the war, Turnley spoke to Kozakiewicz's
father, who had been in one of the first American military units in
Vietnam. Reacting to the censorship of images by military officials, David Kozakiewicz explained that the military was "trying to
make us think this is antiseptic. But this is war. Where is the blood
and the reality of what is happening over there? Finally we have a
picture of what really happens in war." For David Kozakiewicz,
showing his son grieving over the death of a fellow fighter gave
added meaning to the soldier's death.

1 The complete text of Martin Luther King, Jr.'s April 4, 1967, Riverside
   Church speech is posted here:
   www.ratical.org/ratville/JFK/MLKapr67.html

   The speech is also available in the book: *A Testament of Hope: The Essential
   Writings and Speeches of Martin Luther King, Jr.* (HarperSanFrancisco, reprint
   edition, 1990)

INTRODUCTION: HOWARD ZINN

This essay is an edited and expanded version of two earlier articles by

Notes

Howard Zinn, "Support Our Troops: Bring Them Home," *Miami Herald*, January 22, 2005; and "It is not only Iraq that is occupied. America is too," *Guardian* (UK), August 12, 2005.

1 "Grim Realities in Iraq," *New York Times*, December 22, 2004, sec. A, 30.

2 Ibid.

3 Les Roberts, Riyadh Lafta, Richard Garfield, Jamal Khudhairi, and Gilbert Burnham, "Mortality before and after the 2003 invasion of Iraq: Cluster sample survey," *The Lancet*, 364, no. 9448, November 20, 2004, 1857–64.

4 The U.S. military continually reports the total number of U.S. casualties suffered in "Operation Iraqi Freedom" and "Operation Enduring Freedom" on the website: http://www.defenselink.mil/news/casualty.pdf.

5 Michael R. Gordon, "After the War: The Military; To Mollify Iraqis, U.S. Plans to Ease Scope of Its Raids," *New York Times*, August 7, 2003, sec. A, 1.

6 Tom Lasseter and Natalie Pompilio, "Many Iraqis in the Triangle say they've had enough of America's help," Knight Ridder/Tribune News Service—International News, June 17, 2003.

7 For the most current statistics measuring the public's approval/disapproval of President Bush's policy in Iraq see: http://www.pollingreport.com/iraq.htm

8 See www.gulfweb.org/doc_show.cfm?ID=744.

FOREWORD BY HART VIGES

Based on a revised and expanded speech given by Hart Viges on September 21, 2005, at American University.

1 For information about the destructive capacity of a C130 Spectre gunship, see: http://www.fas.org/man/dod-101/sys/ac/ac-130.htm.

Notes

ONE: DEAR PRESIDENT BUSH

1 See the War Resister League's website and get upset about how our tax money is flushed down the military-industrial-complex toilet: http://www.warresisters.org.

   Regarding the U.S. selling death to the world: see Thom Shankar, "Weapon Sales Worldwide Rise to Highest Level Since 2000" *New York Times*, August 30, 2005. The article reports "The value of military weapons sales worldwide jumped in 2004 to the highest level since 2000. . . . The United States once again dominated global weapons sales, signing deals worth $12.4 billion in 2004, or 33.5 percent worldwide." The article is based on a U.S. government report, "Conventional Arms Transfers to Developing Nations," which is posted here: http://www.fas.org/sgp/crs/natsec/RL33051.pdf

2 Mayor Nagin's interview is well worth listening to. CNN has both the text transcript and the sound file posted to their website: http://www.cnn.com/2005/US/09/02/nagin.transcript/

3 Howard Zinn's quote is excerpted from his essay "Just and Unjust War," *The Zinn Reader* (Seven Stories Press, 1997).

4 See Ralph Nader's Open Letter to Cindy Sheehan posted here: http://www.nader.org/template.php?/archives/183-Open-Letter-from-Ralph-Nader-to-Cindy-Sheehan.html

5 The Bush administration's doctrine of preemptive strike is presented in *The National Security Strategy of the United States of America* document posted on the White House website. http://www.whitehouse.gov/nsc/nss.html

6 Comparing the Downing Street memos with what Bush and Blair were telling the public at the time provides primary-source evidence suggesting that the two men purposely and systematically deceived the public in their case for war, and that they had no reasonable plan for achieving stability

nor for rebuilding Iraq after the war. The memos build on earlier memos that state it was "fixing" intelligence information to remove Saddam Hussein months before the war started. A complete copy of the memos along with updates and analysis are available here <www.afterdowningstreet.org>

7 For full text of Charles Duelfer's reports and testimonies see: www.cia.gov/cia/reports/iraq_wmd_2004/ and http://www.cia.gov/cia/public_affairs/speeches/2004/tenet_testimony_03302004.html

8 According to the U.S. military, "Stop Loss is a short-term policy that stabilizes [soldiers] in their current assignment by preventing them from leaving the Corps at the end of their service." See the U.S. Marines website for more:
http://www.usmc.mil/marinelink/mcn2000.nsf/stoploss

9 The complete text of Carly Sheehan's poem, "A Nation Rocked to Sleep," can be found here:
http://www.awakenedwoman.com/casey.htm

10 1,947 U.S. soldiers were killed in "Operation Iraqi Freedom" as of October 7, 2005. Updates are posted daily on the website of the United States Department of Defense.

11 Evidence of President Bush's deteriorating public support can be seen in these polling results: http://www.pollingreport.com/iraq.htm.

12 Here Sheehan refers to her first nights in Crawford when she literally sat in a ditch. For example, see Andrew Gumbel's reference on Common Dreams where he writes "After almost a month of Sheehan mania, the spontaneity that drove Cindy's original act of protest—'one woman walking down a road and sitting in a ditch,' as one organizer, Lauren Sullivan, put it—remains largely intact. Full article here:
http://www.commondreams.org/views05/0901-30.htm where

Notes

13 Since the time of this conversation, Cindy Sheehan has received support from President Hugo Chavez of Venezuela, with whom she met during the 2006 World Social Forum in that country.

14 Congressman Frank Pallone's September 12, 2005, press release reads "Pallone Praises Cindy Sheehan's Efforts to Focus Attention on Iraq War." A complete copy is posted here:
www.house.gov/apps/list/press/nj06_pallone/pr_sept12_Sheehan.html

15 "Taking Stock of the Forever War," *New York Times Magazine*, September 11, 2005. See Mark Danner's website for a complete copy of this fascinating and well-written article:
http://www.markdanner.com/nyt/091105_taking.htm.

THREE: SPEECH AT THE D.C. PROTEST

1 Eric Lipton's articles in the *New York Times* from February 10, 2006, to February 12, 2006 report "In the aftermath of Hurricane Katrina, Bush administration officials said they had been caught by surprise when they were told on Tuesday, Aug. 30, that a levee had broken, allowing floodwaters to engulf New Orleans. But Congressional investigators have now learned that an eyewitness account of the flooding from a federal emergency official reached the Homeland Security Department's headquarters starting at 9:27 p.m. the day before, and the White House itself at midnight." In other words, the White House delayed, and lied about the delay. More than 1,400 people are known to have died along the Gulf Coast as a result of the storm.

FOUR: WARHAWK REPUBLICANS
AND ANTIWAR DEMOCRATS

1 See the National Security Archive webpage "Shaking Hands with Saddam Hussein: The U.S. Tilts toward Iraq, 1980–1984" to see the photograph and video footage of Rumsfeld and Saddam Hussein meeting:
http://www.gwu.edu/ffinsarchiv/NSAEBB/NSAEBB82/

Notes

FIVE: I HAVE ARRIVED, I AM HOME

1 Christian Bible, *Mathew* 6:34.

2 According to the U.S. Department of Veteran Affairs Brief Primer on the
Mental Health Impact of the Wars in Afghanistan and Iraq, "Only one
comprehensive study has examined the mental health impact of the wars
in Afghanistan and Iraq (Hoge et al., 2004). This study evaluated soldiers'
reports of their experiences in the war-zones and reports of symptoms of
psychological distress. The results of this study indicated that the estimated risk for posttraumatic stress disorder (PTSD) from service in the
Iraq War was 18%, and the estimated risk for PTSD from the Afghanistan
mission was 11%." See:
www.ncptsd.va.gov/facts/veterans/fs_iraq_afghanistan_lay_audience.html

SEVEN: SUPPORTING HILLARY

1 See Sarah Ferguson's, "What Hillary Told Cindy Sheehan," *Village Voice*,
September 22, 2005:
http://www.villagevoice.com/news/0539,fergusoncamp,68174,2.html

EIGHT: AFTER MY NEXT ARREST

1 "Iraq requires more sacrifice: Bush," *Herald Sun*, October 26, 2005:
http://www.heraldsun.news.com.au/common/story_page/
0,5478,17039751%255E23109,00.html

NINE: OPEN LETTER TO GEORGE BUSH'S MAMA

1 For an extended transcript of Barbara Bush's comments, see
http://www.underreported.com/modules.php?op=modload&name=
News&file=article&sid=1288&mode=thread&order=0&thold=0

TWELVE: MI FAMILIA DE CORAZÓN

1 One of many excellent organizations that provide information about

Notes

becoming a conscientious objector is the Central Committee for
Conscientious Objectors. Check out their website:
http://www.objector.org/

THIRTEEN: COMFORT ZONES

1 Brain Haw's website may be accessed here:
http://www.parliament-square.org.uk/index.htm

FIFTEEN: THE OPPOSITE OF GOOD IS APATHY

1 Bush's estimate that at least 30,000 civilians had been killed in Iraq as of
December 12, 2005 was widely reported, as in this article from the *Seattle
Times*:
http://seattletimes.nwsource.com/html/nationworld/
2002680398_bushiraq13.html

Other sources report that the number at the time was much higher . . .
perhaps higher than 100,000 civilians killed, as in this piece broadcast by
Amy Goodman's *Democracy Now*, "Study Shows Civilian Death Toll in Iraq
More Than 100,000." For a transcript of the broadcast, see:
http://www.democracynow.org/article.pl?sid=05/12/14/154251.

SEVENTEEN: ANOTHER WORLD IS POSSIBLE

1 Excerpted from a transcript of a sermon that Martin Luther King, Jr. delivered at Ebenezer Baptist Church in Atlanta, Georgia, on February 4, 1968.
A complete transcript is posted here:
http://www.stanford.edu/group/King/publications/
sermons/680204.000_Drum_Major_Instinct.html

More Information

GOLD STAR FAMILIES FOR PEACE

An organization of the families of soldiers who have died as a result of war, organizing to be a positive force in our world to bring our country's sons and daughters home from Iraq, to minimize the "human cost" of this war, and to prevent other families from the pain we are feeling as the result of our losses.

contact@gsfp.org

www.gsfp.org

MILITARY FAMILIES SPEAK OUT

An organization of people who are opposed to war in Iraq and who have relatives or loved ones in the military. They were formed in November 2002 and have contacts with military families throughout the United States and in other countries around the world.

P.O. Box 549

Jamaica Plain, MA 02130

(617) 983-0710

mfso@mfso.org

www.mfso.org

IRAQ VETERANS AGAINST THE WAR

Iraq Veterans Against the War went public on July 28, 2004. The main objectives of IVAW are threefold. They are: 1: Bring the troops home now; 2: Support Iraqi reconstruction in whatever way possible; 3: Support our veterans and our troops now and upon their return home.

More Information

P.O. Box 8296
Philadelphia, PA 19101
(215) 241-7123
ivaw@ivaw.net
www.ivaw.net

CENTRAL COMMITTEE FOR CONSCIENTIOUS OBJECTORS

The Central Committee for Conscientious Objectors has been in existence continuously since 1948, helping people who get caught in the military's web and helping them get out. Programs include: Military Out of Our Schools, the GI Rights Hotline, Third World Outreach Program, and AWOL! Youth for Peace and Revolution.

405 14th Street #205
Oakland, CA 94612
(888) 236-2226
info@objector.org
www.objector.org

CODEPINK

CODEPINK is a women-initiated grassroots peace and social justice movement that seeks positive social change through proactive, creative protest and nonviolent direct action.. There are more than eighty active CODEPINK communities. CODE-PINK-Central serves to connect CODEPINK groups with the international network of global peacemakers.

2010 Linden Ave
Venice, CA 90291

More Information

(310) 827-4320
info@codepinkalert.org
www.codepink4peace.org

VETERANS FOR PEACE

VFP is a national organization that includes men and women veterans from World War II, Korea, Vietnam, the Gulf War, other conflicts, and peacetime veterans. We draw on our personal experiences and perspectives gained as veterans to raise public awareness of the true costs and consequences of militarism and war, and to seek peaceful, effective alternatives.

216 South Meramec Avenue
St. Louis, MO 63105
(314) 725-6005
vfp@igc.org
www.veteransforpeace.org

AFTERDOWNINGSTREET.ORG

Leads a campaign to urge the U.S. Congress to begin a formal investigation into whether President Bush has committed impeachable offenses in connection with the Iraq war. Join our coalition!

www.afterdowningstreet.org

U.S. MILITARY

The U.S. military posts daily updates of the total number of U.S. soldiers killed in Iraq and Afghanistan.

To see the lastest tragic number go to:
www.defenselink.mil/news/casualty.pdf

Cindy Sheehan is the internationally known mom and peace and social justice advocate whose son, Army Specialist Casey A. Sheehan, was killed in action in Sadr City, Baghdad, on April 4, 2004. Cindy Sheehan is founder of Gold Star Families for Peace, an organization of Americans who have had loved ones killed in wars. As an act of protest against the war, in August 2005 Cindy took a stand outside of George Bush's home in Crawford, Texas, asking what noble cause her son died for; this began the Camp Casey peace camp movement. She is author of *Not One More Mother's Child* (Koa Books) and *Peace Mom* (forthcoming from Simon and Schuster.)

Howard Zinn grew up in the immigrant slums of Brooklyn, where he worked in shipyards in his late teens. He saw combat duty as an air force bombardier in World War II; afterward he received his doctorate in history from Columbia University and was a postdoctoral fellow in East Asian Studies at Harvard University. His first book, *La Guardia in Congress*, was an Albert Beveridge Prize winner. He is the author of numerous books, including his epic masterpiece, *A People's History of the United States*. A professor emeritus of political science at Boston University, Zinn lives with his wife, Roslyn, in the Boston area, near their children and grandchildren.

Hart Viges is an Iraq war veteran, peace advocate, and public speaker. Hart served in the 82nd Airborne Division and was deployed to Iraq from February 2003 to January 2004. After returning home, Hart applied for and was awarded conscientious objector status ten months later and was released from the army. Viges also spent time at Camp Casey and is the chairman of the Austin, Texas, chapter of Iraq Veterans Against the War.